Seven Secrets of Mindfulness

Seven Secrets of Mindfulness

How to Keep Your Everyday Practice Alive

Kate Carne

LONDON • SYDNEY • AUCKLAND • JOHANNESBURG

1 3 5 7 9 10 8 6 4 2

Rider, an imprint of Ebury Publishing,
20 Vauxhall Bridge Road,
London SW1V 2SA

Rider is part of the Penguin Random House group of companies whose
addresses can be found at global.penguinrandomhouse.com

Copyright © Kate Carne 2016

First published by Rider in 2016

www.penguin.co.uk

A CIP catalogue record for this book is available from the British Library

ISBN 9781846045042

Typeset in India by Thomson Digital Pvt Ltd, Noida, Delhi

Printed and bound in Great Britain by Clays Ltd, St Ives plc

Penguin Random House is committed to a sustainable future for our
business, our readers and our planet. This book is made from Forest
Stewardship Council® certified paper.

For those who long
to discover
their inner path

May their practice
ripple out
to benefit all beings
and this precious earth

For their wise help with this book,
namaste
to Brigid Avison,
Jonas Torrance, Barbara Bender,
John Torrance, Ursula Harrison,
Jenny Haxworth, Chris Cullen, Sabina Cardoso
and Susan Lascelles.

For their inspired teaching,
namaste
to Hogen Daido Yamahata,
Thich Nhat Hanh, Mark Williams,
Ferris Urbanoski, Jon Kabat-Zinn
and Brigid Avison.

Special thanks to all those
mindfulness students
who shared their stories –
they are true teachers.

Contents

List of Illustrations   xi
Introduction   xiii

The First Secret: Lighting the Inner Fire
1. Building the fire   3
2. Feeling the heat   6
3. Gathering the fuel   10
4. Breathing life into the fire   17

The Second Secret: Mapping the Obstacle Course
5. Introducing obstacles   23
6. Physical obstacles   25
7. Attachments and desires   34
8. Aversion   42
9. Depression   51
10. Unhelpful views   58

The Third Secret: Understanding the Roots of Resistance
11. Working with resistance: the first key   63
12. Working with resistance: the second key   66

The Fourth Secret: Understanding How to Practise
13. Three essentials   73
14. Effort and ease   77
15. The toolkit   87
16. About breathing   114
17. What goes on in the mind   121

The Fifth Secret: Understanding that Support is Vital
18. Finding the support we need   129

Contents

The Sixth Secret: Seeing the Path All Around

19. Signposts   139

The Seventh Secret: Entering the Dragon Gate

20. The Dragon Gate   155
21. After-story (within a story)   158

Acknowledgements   162
Notes   163
Further reading   167
About the author   169
Index   170

We never regret the time we spend practising.[1]

– Neville Dowley

List of Illustrations

Figure 1. Life's spiral and experiences of depression   53

Figure 2. The historical and the ultimate dimensions   69

Figure 3. Three sitting positions   93

Figure 4. Positions for the hands   96

Figure 5. The diaphragm   118

Figure 6. Two models of the mind during meditation   124

Introduction

Mindfulness is a wonderful practice. If you are reading this, then perhaps you have already experienced the spaciousness that arises when your awareness is focusing on *this* moment. When we offer ourselves the opportunity to pay attention, we discover a new world. Sensations, thoughts, emotions, sounds – all of these inform us that our experience is rich and unique and ever-changing. As we pay attention, our curiosity grows, and curiosity helps us let go of judging. An open mind means that we lose the urge to jump to conclusions. Instead, we realise that we have freedom to choose how to respond, what to say, and even which view we take of a situation. The path of mindfulness offers greater appreciation of life, more happiness, less suffering, and even better sleep. And so the question arises, as one student put it: *'Given that I know how much mindfulness has helped me, why do I find it so difficult to practise?'*

This is the question that this book aims to investigate.

Resistance is a factor that comes up for everyone who attempts to undertake meditative practice. The word 'practice' is the key: no one ever genuinely understood or benefited from mindfulness just by reading a book or listening to a lecture on the subject. *Mindfulness is a practice.* Not only that, but it is meant to be a *regular* practice. This point is illustrated beautifully in an interview given by Jon Kabat-Zinn, who first developed the Mindfulness-Based Stress Reduction programme at the University of Massachusetts Medical Centre in the late 1970s.

He was asked if mindfulness could just be a 'Band-Aid' – in other words, something that we use occasionally, in moments of need. Kabat-Zinn replied:

> Mindfulness is definitely not a Band-Aid.
> Meditation is like weaving a parachute. You don't want to start weaving the parachute when you're about to jump out of the plane. You want to have been weaving the parachute morning, noon and night, day in and day out, and then when you need it, it might actually hold you. And so the way we practise meditation is to do it every day – to carve out some time each day that's just your time for being.[1]

These days, people who attend a mindfulness course appreciate that practice is part of the package. In fact, often they attend a course after attempting to learn mindfulness from a book. Perhaps they have even tried listening to the CD that accompanies many mindfulness books – if so, the most common experience that people report is, 'I tried to do the practice on my own, but it was difficult.'

If you have had the good fortune to attend a mindfulness course, you will probably have discovered that going to class does make practising easier. Having a real person guide us through a meditation captures the attention in a way that a recording cannot. Practising with a group of other people who are also engaged in paying attention creates a supportive environment, and a sense of shared experience. Practising at home alone is still challenging, but most participants start off with good intentions. Some mindfulness students are immediately eager and committed, but others, whenever they consider practising, come up against a roadblock. This roadblock can take many forms: there are external obstacles, such as a deadline at work, illness, holiday, or even the dog that continuously licks your face every time you lie down on the floor to practise. And then there are the internal ones: boredom, restlessness, doubt, exhaustion, and often simply the feeling that there are other, more important things to do. Some mindfulness students find a way to negotiate their roadblocks; others do not. Those who do not will limp through the rest of the course, feeling a bit guilty, judging themselves harshly, chalking up mindfulness on the same list along with all of those failed diets and exercise regimes that would have changed their lives, if only they could stick to them.

Obstacles to practice are nothing new. Teachings were created on this subject more than two millennia ago for Buddhist monks. These obstacles were called 'hindrances', and it was said that so long as these hindrances were not abandoned, the monks would be 'Indebted, ailing, imprisoned, enslaved, and travelling in a wilderness'.[2] Clearly not a desirable state! The five hindrances they were warned about are:

- sensual desire
- ill will
- sloth and torpor
- remorse and restlessness
- doubt

Remedies were prescribed for each of these afflictions. For example, one way for a monk to overcome sensual desire for a lovely young woman was to imagine her body once it was dead and decaying. One of the ways to get rid of torpor was to avoid overeating. And ill will, the teachings say, can be transformed through loving-kindness meditation.

It's a deeply thoughtful list of hindrances, with practical suggestions for overcoming each one. And yet, when I began to teach mindfulness in 2004, and would try (in my own mind) to relate students' problems to these ancient teachings, there often seemed to be a gap. This is partly because both the hindrances and their remedies were aimed at people living in a monastic community. People on modern mindfulness courses are not monks, and therefore their orientation is different. But it is also because our modern dilemmas include expectations and distractions (such as our smartphones) that no one had even dreamt of 2,500 years ago. Therefore, in order to support mindfulness students in the twenty-first century, it seemed that a new consideration of hindrances might be helpful.

Over the years, mindfulness students have repeatedly taught me that hindrances, obstacles, roadblocks – call them what you will – are the big issue. They are the knot that all mindfulness practitioners need to know how to untie if they are to keep their practice alive. Without practice, mindfulness does not exist. While the traditional texts on hindrances are interesting, the humble intention of this book is to provide an update. It is not a matter of reinventing the wheel – rather, the aim is to add a few new spokes. This book will do its best to investigate both the kinds of hindrances that we are likely to face in the midst of our busy lives, and the approaches that we need in order to negotiate them.

Taking a mindful view, the secret to working with the resistances we encounter is to examine them. We need to understand their size, their purpose, their texture, their roots. Only through this approach of being intimate with them – in fact allowing this examination of the roadblocks to *become* our mindfulness practice – can we hope to stop struggling with them or finding ourselves completely overwhelmed by the obstacles they present. To quote a children's song:[3]

We can't go under it,
We can't go around it,
We have to go through it.

When resistance arises, we need to learn how to move through it. Moving through can only truly occur when we meet and befriend our obstacles with deep awareness. This book offers some thoughts on what that means, and on how to do it skilfully, with the chance to be present for each courageous step that we take along the way.

There is one thing in this world which must never be forgotten. If you were to forget everything else, but were not to forget this, there would be no cause for worry.

While if you remembered, performed and attended to everything else, but forgot that one thing, you would in fact have done nothing whatsoever.

It is as if a king had sent you to a country to carry out one special, specific task. You go to the country, and you perform a hundred other tasks, but not the task you have been sent for; it is as if you have performed nothing at all.

So we have come into the world for a particular task, and that is our purpose. If we don't perform it, we have done nothing at all.

Rumi[4]

**The
First
Secret**

Lighting the
Inner Fire

1.
Building the fire

Today the hut is cold. These two hands make a bed of crumpled newspaper in the small wood burner, tear up cardboard to go on top, add some twigs, and crown the arrangement with two fatter branches. The newspaper takes up the fire from the match, and passes it on to the cardboard. But now there is a problem. The kindling twigs are damp – gathered too soon after the rain. They hold their moisture, and do not succumb to the heat. Because they do not catch fire, neither do the larger branches on top of them. The fire goes out ... it is cold enough to see the breath.

Creating a mindfulness practice is a lot like building a fire. Without the right elements, introduced at the right moments, and in the right proportions, it does not take. If you are reading this book, then perhaps you have made some kind of effort to get going with your practice, only to be met with one or more seemingly insurmountable obstacles. So although you tried, you were left with a cold hearth, a discouraged mind, and the sense that either mindfulness is not the miracle cure that it's cracked up to be, or that you are inadequate and have failed in some way.

To create fire, three elements are required: fuel, heat and oxygen. The paper, the kindling, the wood may all be perfectly arranged, but if there is no match, there is no heat to get the fire going. Or perhaps we have the matches and dry logs, but no paper or kindling – no matter how long we hold the flame to the logs, the flame from one small match will not ignite them. Or we have all of the elements we need, and light the paper, and then just close the door and the vents to the wood burner ... without the extra breath of air from the bellows, the fire goes out.

The more practice we have in building a fire, the more in tune we are with what it needs. We get to know how much newspaper is required, and what twigs will make good kindling. We can tell from the weight of a log whether it is dry enough to burn. We can listen to the sounds of the flames and know if there is enough air, or hear the creaking of the stove and know that it is heating up.

In meditation practice the same sort of elements are required.

Heat (discomfort)

Something needs to ignite the intention to take on this new practice. Usually the heat arises from suffering. Something about our lives is not comfortable – perhaps we are in physical pain, or emotional pain, or perhaps all that we have to do is making us feel stressed out and frazzled. We need to be clear about why we are practising in order for the fire to burn bright. Understanding *why I want to practise* (because of this suffering) is crucial, because without clarity about this *why*, it's unlikely that practice will be maintained. Discomfort is the heat that lights the fire and gets us going.

Fuel (mindful practices)

The wood burner needs wood – this is the form that holds the fire, off which it feeds. With mindfulness practice, the fuel that we use consists of the specific practices that we learn: the body scan, seated meditation, kindness, the breathing space, etc. (See page 87 on 'The toolkit' for more about these.) Choosing the wrong practice is a bit like having damp kindling – the fire goes out. So knowing which practice will be most suitable at any given moment takes some training, a bit like building the fire. If the first fire you lay goes out, then it's important to start again with other materials.

Oxygen (intention)

How much oxygen we feed a fire will determine whether it lives or dies. And once the fire is established, controlling the flow of air will control the rate at which the wood burns. In mindfulness practice, the oxygen that breathes life into the meditation is our intention, our will, our dedication. We already appreciate that we want to make changes to how we live so that we suffer less, but this intellectual understanding alone is not enough. We need to collect our energy together and focus our will and determination to carve out the time and space and attention that is required to actually practise. This is where intention is critical. It is our understanding and our will coming together that makes mindfulness practice possible. So long as we lack intention, like a fire starved of oxygen, our practice will fizzle out. Developing and maintaining a clear and manageable intention is the key that makes it possible to begin to practise, and also enables us to negotiate whatever obstacles we encounter along the way.

2.
Feeling the heat

Building another nest of paper and cardboard. In the bottom of the log basket, there are a few dry twigs. This time, because the bellows blow in extra oxygen, the initial flames grow in heat and confidence. And now the sound of crackling – a sign that the twigs have caught the heat. One more blow of the bellows, and the fire is alight.

It is difficult to accept suffering. Nobody wants it, nobody is immune. We spend a great deal of our time and energy organising our lives to minimise our discomfort, but in the end it is always here. Human beings have achieved, built, created, thought and dreamt the most astonishing things, and yet we have not by-passed pain and dissatisfaction. In fact, our imaginations, in pondering how we might improve on the status quo, tend to intensify the sense that things are not sufficient as they are – and that we are not sufficient either – all of which increases our suffering. Add to that the fragility of the human body, subject as it is to ill health, old age and death, and it becomes clear that none of us can avoid pain and suffering.

As you read this, the inevitability of suffering is probably the last thing you want to hear. If you are interested in mindfulness, it may well be due to a desire to ease pain, to reduce stress: in other words, to use mindfulness as a tool to be free of suffering. This search puts us in good company: 2,500 years ago, a young man, when confronted for the first time by someone who was old, another who was ill, and yet another who had just died, decided that he must find a way to overcome human misery. He spent years searching out various teachers, trying different techniques, but nothing he discovered answered his question about the way to overcome suffering. Finally, he left everyone behind and went off on his own. A local girl brought him some rice to eat, which he gratefully accepted. When his fellow ascetic monks heard this, they judged that he was weak and no longer a worthy friend.

The young man resolved to sit under the tree until he had solved the terrible problem of human suffering. This might sound a bit strange – if we're worried about other people, isn't it better to *do* something? But the young man realised that he needed to begin with understanding. Without understanding the *why,* he knew he could not reveal the *how: how can this suffering be overcome?*

Perhaps you know by now that this is the story of the Buddha. Buddha means 'one who is awake'. He was not any kind of God, nor did he speak of God. He was a human being, just like you and me.

What this young man realised early one morning was this:

- There is suffering in the world.
- There are reasons that we suffer (desire, aversion, ignorance).
- There is a way out of suffering.
- The way out of suffering is by following what he described as an eight-fold path in life, which includes having skilful views, skilful thoughts, skilful speech, skilful actions, skilful effort, skilful concentration, skilful mindfulness and an appropriate livelihood.[1]

Simple, isn't it? Although these days mindfulness is taught in a non-spiritual context as a series of practical tools, it is helpful to appreciate its origins: one young man, several hundred years ago in northern India, who wanted to understand and alleviate the suffering of all of us.

In essence, our own journey is not much different. We find ourselves in the midst of a life that is sometimes difficult, and often feels beyond our control. We know that we need to find a better way to cope, but whatever other methods we may have tried seem to offer only temporary relief or distraction. And then we read an article, or hear something on the radio, about something called mindfulness. We know it's going to involve time and effort. Inevitably, there is hesitation. This hesitation is useful – we are considering, but not yet ready to commit. At some point desperation takes over; we are so depressed, or so anxious, or in such pain, that we know we must find a different way to live. Our desperation is the key that makes transformation possible. Our suffering gives us a licence to let go of things that are making us worse; our suffering is what makes us willing to change how we live. Without suffering, there would be no heat, and no liberation, as this story from Lucy, who attended a mindfulness course, illustrates:

A few years ago, I was diagnosed with cancer. One day I was rushing from work to pick my kids up and wondering what to feed them for supper, the next day I was faced with my own death. It was like I'd been sleepwalking, and suddenly, I had to wake up. I didn't know how much longer I would live. I didn't know how much longer my children would have a mother – that was the hardest part. I'm usually a great planner, making sure that everything goes well, and there I was, faced with the reality that I was not in control. I did all the treatments, changed my diet, and cut back on work – and I started to realise that having cancer meant that not only did I have to make changes, but that I actually wanted to make them. I wanted, for the first time, not to be in a rush. After all, what was I rushing towards – the day when I would no longer be here? A friend suggested mindfulness, so I went on a course and learnt how to meditate. For that bit of time each day, I got the hang of not thinking about the future. I actually found that I could enjoy the present, even when it seemed like nothing was happening. I let go of a lot. I started to listen more deeply to my children, to just spend time with them – because I realised that it was so precious. Of course I still get tired, and cross, and anxious, but I have also learnt to be present and to really appreciate this life that I have been given. Now, looking back on things, I sometimes think that having cancer has actually made my life better.*

Lucy's experience is a lesson for all of us. We don't generally let go of things until we are forced to. And yet, in the letting go, we are able to experience more spaciousness, greater freedom, and the possibility of being truly alive.

* At the time of writing, Lucy is well.

3.
Gathering the fuel

Sunlight shines in low through the bare branches of willow. Today, arriving at the woodpile with an axe. Some logs give to the blade easier than others – choosing the ones that feel light for their size. Chopping involves not thinking, but looking: looking at the place on the thin end of the log where the axe must land. With each swing there is a little more confidence, and the satisfying thwack of the blade cutting one piece into two. Pale tree flesh that has never seen daylight is suddenly exposed. Soon, there is a large basket full of kindling: perfect treasure.

If you have attended a mindfulness course, you will know that the underlying principle is to weave regular practice into your daily life. This approach is one of deep wisdom. It is relatively easy to go off on retreat, feel fired up about meditation practice, and then have it all fall away like sand disappearing through our fingers once we are back in the midst of a busy life. One of the great gifts of a weekly class is that we are embedding practice into our ordinary lives from the very beginning. This gives us a much better chance of working out how we can maintain awareness in the midst of any situation.

On a mindfulness course, students are given various practices. This means that by the end of an eight-week course, there are long as well as short practices that we can use, according to need and time. As mentioned in Chapter 1, the trick is in knowing how to choose. This is a bit like being our own physician: understanding our condition, and selecting the appropriate remedy. (For more on specific practices, see page 87, Chapter 15.)

Habit energy

The 'condition' that afflicts most people most of the time is called 'habit energy'. Habit energy is what drives us when we are not fully conscious of our actions – a kind of autopilot that can steer us through life without our being fully awake or in control. Usually this habit energy involves some form of 'doing' – whether it's mental or physical. Our habit energy might be to surf the net, to check our phone, to fill our diary, to plan the next meal. It might involve imaginary conversations in the mind, or monologues justifying our actions. It might be cleaning, or worrying about our children, restlessness, eating, problem-solving, anxiety, drinking, anger or procrastination. Each of us has our forms of habitual energy, and understanding which mindful practice might be most beneficial involves asking the question, 'What's going on within me right now?' In other words, we bring into the full light of awareness what has been lurking in the shadows.

Pausing, observing, choosing

Most people in the modern world spend much of their time focused on mental activity. We are constantly thinking about what we have to do (the future) or about what we have done (the past). As mindfulness students, our first task is to recognise what's going on in the mind; in other words, to be able to observe our habit energy. Realising what our minds are up to is the first step towards becoming free.

Out of this realisation, we can create an opportunity to pause. And from pausing, we begin to have choices about how to proceed. If the mind is going around in circles like a hamster on a wheel, simply to pause is a wonderful experience. And to feel that there might be a choice as to what to do next – this is nothing short of miraculous.

Pausing and observing: these are the beginnings of mindfulness. The moment we notice what the mind is doing, *we are already in the present moment.* In the simple act of becoming aware, we begin to have the tools to build our fire. The pausing and noticing are like the bits of scrunched-up newspaper: they are the foundations that will make the fire viable, as Clara's story demonstrates:

> The other day, my husband and I started to have an argument. Usually one of us will say something that irritates the other, and before you know it we are having a shouting match. So my husband said something that annoyed me, and I could feel the anger rising, and I realised at that moment that I didn't have to react. I didn't have to start arguing. So I didn't. I could see him looking at me, almost waiting for the explosion. But it didn't happen. I took some deep breaths. I realised that I felt in control. My husband couldn't quite figure out what was going on. It felt wonderful.

Kindling

Mindfulness practice can, at the beginning, seem somewhat daunting. Taking on a thirty- or forty-five-minute practice in the midst of an already busy life is a big ask. For many of us, although we may be relatively well off in other ways, we live in deep poverty when it comes to time. This is the most common refrain on a mindfulness course: *'There wasn't enough time.'* We struggle to get ourselves (and possibly our children) ready for work (and school) each day. We struggle through traffic and commuting to get to work on time. We struggle to meet deadlines, to get through appraisals, to please our bosses and the other people we work with. And then we struggle to get home again, to sort out food, to make sure there are clean clothes for the next day, to keep our homes in some sort of order. Although your own scenario will differ in some ways, the refrain is likely to be the same: *There isn't enough time to get everything done.*

If this is how it is, then adding another commitment may appear to be foolhardy. But it can be done. Here is the story of Adam:

To be honest, my wife signed me up for this course. I run a small business, so I work long hours, and always worry about the finances – about being able to keep my employees on, and having enough money for my family. When I was on the course, if we did the body scan, I just fell asleep. I never really managed the long home practices; it would have involved getting up earlier, and I was just too tired. But I did really pay attention to brushing my teeth. I know it doesn't sound like much, but for those two minutes, I just brushed my teeth. It gave my mind a rest – I stopped thinking about work – and made my teeth cleaner too. In the first weeks I felt like the course was just another thing I wasn't doing well enough, but part way through I began to see that the stress I felt (about almost everything) was not intrinsic in the situation: it arose from the way I was thinking. By the end of the course my blood pressure was ten points lower than it had been at the beginning. It made me realise that even small changes we make to how we think and do things can have a big impact on our lives.

Adam's story demonstrates how anyone – no matter how busy and pressured – can become more mindful. It also shows how even a short practice can be beneficial. But most importantly, Adam teaches us how, in becoming aware of the habit energy of the mind, he was able to change his stress levels and lower his blood pressure. This numerical, objective evidence is invaluable, because it lessens doubt, and it also means that Adam will be more likely to carry on with his practice.

To use our fire-building analogy, Adam found the right sort of kindling. Bringing awareness to a daily activity meant that he didn't need to find any extra time to practise – he simply turned his attention to something he was doing anyway. So instead of brushing his teeth while thinking about all the things he had to do at work that day, he just paid attention to the sound, the taste, the sensation of brushing his teeth. Instead of brushing mindlessly, Adam brushed with attention – which is to say, he brought his awareness into the present moment. He went from being scattered – his body doing one thing while his mind was thinking about something else – to being whole, in this moment. It sounds so easy, and it is. The intention to be present and whole is what allows us to unearth the true treasure of our lives.

Adding bigger logs

Once the kindling has caught fire, it's sensible to add larger pieces of wood. This means the fire will burn for longer, and also that it will give off more warmth. In terms of mindfulness, these bigger logs are the longer, thirty- or forty-minute practices that are offered, such as the body scan and seated meditation. But if you've tried a full-length practice, it's likely that you will have encountered various challenges. Perhaps the mind does not really want to pay attention to the breath; instead it keeps wandering back to all of the items on its 'To Do' list. Perhaps the body feels restless and uncomfortable. Perhaps bubbles come to the surface in the mind or the emotions – bubbles that you are doing your best to avoid. All of these disturbances are basically saying, 'Stop doing this meditation – let's get on with something else, something easier, something more productive.' After all, Adam's story suggests that we might see a significant change just from how we brush our teeth. So why spend half an hour doing nothing?

The autonomic nervous system

In order to answer this question, it's helpful to know a bit about human physiology. In our bodies, we have a wonderful function called the autonomic nervous system. Autonomic essentially means that it is automatic – it does its job without any direction from us. We don't have to think about our heart beating or our lungs taking in each new breath – it all just happens naturally.

Within the autonomic nervous system, there are two operating modes. The first mode, called the para-sympathetic nervous system, regulates the way our bodies function when we are at rest. Our heart beats slowly, our breathing is slow, we can digest our food, we feel at ease. Let's call this para-sympathetic mode the green light.

The other operating mode is for when we feel threatened. This is called the sympathetic nervous system, and when this kicks into action, we are on high alert. Breathing and heart rate quicken, we feel stronger, we are in 'fight or flight' mode.[1]

When we're stressed, the sympathetic side of the nervous system is switched on – let's call it the red light. It makes us feel aggressive or panicky.

One of things we may notice when we sit (or lie) down to practise is that we are feeling stressed. Through paying attention to the body and the breath, bringing ourselves to the present moment, the stress levels may diminish. This switching, from the sympathetic (red light) to the para-sympathetic (green light), takes time. For most people, the shift from red to green takes around twenty minutes. Once you understand this, you begin to appreciate why it's so important to engage with the longer practices. If you only ever try a three- or ten-minute practice, you never fully experience what it means to step out of *doing* and into *being*, as this story demonstrates:

One time a teacher was explaining to her class the fact that it takes about twenty minutes for the body (and mind) to move out of 'doing mode' and into a state of greater ease. A student then asked, 'If it takes twenty minutes, then why does the practice you've given us last for thirty minutes. Why can't we stop after twenty?'

The teacher reflected for a moment and then replied, 'Well … why would you want to?'

4.
Breathing life into the fire

This morning, less than a month to midwinter, the first frost clings to the edges of each leaf like fine lace. Through the trees the air looks filled with smoke, but actually it is steam rising from the damp forest floor as the sunlight touches it. The trees drip, the last leaves fall, a deep, dank smell rises from wet earth. Today, with the newly split logs, the fire lights instantly.

We know that we are suffering in some way, and we are fortunate in that we have discovered a book or class offering mindfulness practices. There is just one more step we have to take – we need to create intention, so that we actually take time out from our daily activities, locate the body scan, and press 'play'. Not only that, we need to turn the phone off, and to focus fully on listening to the words. These may seem like small steps, but they are also the giant leap that moves us from *thinking* about mindfulness to actually beginning to *practise*.

Intention is the air that we breathe into our mindfulness hearth. Without it, even a well-laid fire will not burn. Particularly at the beginning, the fire needs extra air, or the heat that shows red on the edge of the paper will not burst into flame. Air quickens the fire, and helps it to move from the paper to the kindling, from the kindling to the larger pieces of wood. Too much air, and the fire burns too quickly, or can even be blown out. Not enough air, and we are doomed to sit in the cold. The air that we feed into the fire needs to be continuous and steady, or the flames will be extinguished. It's much easier to keep the fire going than to let it go out and have to start again from scratch. The same is true of mindfulness practice: steady input is the key to developing the warm internal glow of awareness.

Intention is formed from the question that arose earlier in the pages about heat and suffering. The question is: *why am I doing this? Why am I interested in mindfulness, and what do I wish to gain from it?* Without clarity about the answers to these questions, intention will falter.

People attend mindfulness courses for many reasons: stress, anxiety, depression, ill health, pain, the desire to be a better parent or spouse, the wish to be more effective at work, or simply the desire to be more peaceful and present. Most of us take up mindfulness practice to make our lives better in some way. Mindfulness is a tool we learn to use for our personal benefit. This is one of the main ways that secular mindfulness differs from that practised within a spiritual paradigm: in the Buddhist view, mindfulness is practised to enable people to realise their connection to, and their compassion towards, the whole world.

No matter whether we are attempting to deal with the personal or the universal, the issue of suffering remains a key point. For people in considerable pain, or with a life-limiting illness, the suffering is all too clear. Therefore, their intention is clear: *I need to find some way of making this situation/pain bearable.* The distraction and suppression that they might have once used to block out their discomfort no longer work, and it comes down to the fact that, in essence, there is no alternative. Desperation creates heat and urgency, which in turn clarifies intention. They cannot forget about their reason for wanting to practise, because their body is telling them, in each moment, that it's in pain. These people, although their pain may make it difficult for them to get to the class, will do much better on the course than someone who comes along out of a general interest, or because his spouse thought it would be a good idea. The clearer and more insistent our pain is, the clearer and stronger our resolve.

How many New Year's resolutions have you made in your lifetime? How many have you kept? Probably the more successful ones will have been time-limited – so, for example, giving up alcohol or chocolate for the month of January is more achievable than giving it up for ever. In approaching mindfulness practice, this attitude is also helpful. If you set yourself the goal of practising every day for the whole of the course, then quite possibly at some point you will fail.

This is why, on the mindfulness courses, the very first invitation is often to be non-judgmental. If I don't manage to practise today, can I still be kind to myself? Or if I sit, and my mind is continually jumping from one topic to the next, can I refrain from beating myself up? Can I let go of the notion of 'failure' and instead just be curious about whatever is arising? As Ajahn Sucitto, a Theravada monk from the Chithurst Forest Monastery in West Sussex, says; 'Success *and* failure, when carried out with good intention, both lead to wisdom, peace and kindness.'[1] This means that no matter how unsuccessful we may judge ourselves to be at practice, the fact that we are trying, in whatever way we can manage, means that there will be benefit – specifically, wisdom, peace and kindness. Once we realise this, the habit energy of judging becomes less insistent.

Finally, there is a key question, and within it is the secret we need to reveal in order to clarify intention, and it is this:

What is my deepest wish?

Pause, and reflect on this ...

What do you really want, for yourself, and people that you know, and the world?

It may not be anything that you can easily put into words.

It may not even be a question that you can answer at this moment.

But keep the question within you.

It is a question that illuminates the secret of practice.

It is like the needle on your inner compass that will orientate you, and help you to walk on your path.

When that path is clear, your reason for practising meditation will also become clear.

And when the path and the reason are clear, practice arises as our commitment to living this one precious life that we have been given, as well as we can.

So, what is your deepest wish?

The Second Secret

Mapping the Obstacle Course

5.
Introducing obstacles

Today, after lighting the fire, taking time to go outside and fill the feeders. On returning to the hut, the hearth is cold. But not even any embers. It gets so cold in here at night that the locks freeze, and the wood is just too chilled to accept the flames. Here is the choice: start again, or retreat. Pausing ... Now these chilled hands arrange more paper, more kindling – no longer any thought of doing this in order to then do something else. Just determined to coax this one small fire into existence.

What a lot of reasons we can find to avoid practising! Over the years students have listed dozens of kinds of resistance, perhaps imagining that if they could only overcome the one hurdle that seems to be blocking their path, everything else would suddenly be easy. But it's a curious fact about obstacles: when one disappears, another tends to rise up on the track in front of us. The image of a hurdle race is useful here: the expert runner knows that there are a series of fences to negotiate, and so she measures her paces in order to meet each hurdle with enough bounce to avoid being tripped up. In fact, without the hurdles, there would be no event. This is the same for us as mindfulness students: we need to accept that there will be obstacles, and that these obstacles can become part of our practice, rather than getting in the way of it. As Jon Kabat-Zinn so skilfully put it in one of his lectures, 'Whatever is going on in your life is the curriculum.'[1] Whatever we are facing is what we need to deal with right now, so *this* is the centre of our practice.

Mindfulness means intimacy. When there is an obstacle, our unconscious tendency may well be to turn away; but in fact the secret is to move in close, and become familiar with the barrier that stands before us. What follows in this section is a list of the most common roadblocks that arise. You are unlikely to experience all of them, but inevitably there are some that you will know very well. And knowing what is going on is the first step to figuring out how to negotiate whatever the obstacle might be.

6.
Physical obstacles

Suddenly, with small fast movements, a squirrel appears in front of the hut. A plastic dome keeps him from getting to the bird feeders, but he's found a peanut on the ground. With tiny articulate paws he grabs the nut and sits up, nibbling furiously, his tail curled up along his back in a question mark.

The body is miraculous. It transforms food into energy, and endlessly performs complex and interrelated activities of which we have only the faintest notion. It gives us mobility, thought, a wealth of sensation, and enables us to experience and appreciate the world. But when this complex organism goes awry, we may well feel pain and frustration. These can present serious obstacles to practising meditation. In this chapter, we'll look at the obstacles that arise due to physical suffering, and also examine how to approach these obstacles in a mindful way. Please feel free to dip into the parts of this section that feel the most relevant to you.

Illness

Illness falls mainly into two categories: the acute ones, like flu, which can incapacitate us for a time, and from which we recover; and the more chronic forms of ill health that may drag on for years. Acute illness, particularly the kind that keeps us in bed, is going to interfere with any urge we have to mindfulness practice, as the illness is affecting both body and mind. Often during an acute illness, we have to let go of our normal routines, accept that we can't go to work, and put most things on hold until we're feeling better.

Chronic illness differs from acute in that we tend, in some restricted way perhaps, to carry on with daily life – but the illness makes everything much more difficult. Emotional factors may enter in here: we may despair of recovery, or feel that we just don't have the capacity to carry on. Chronic illness may actually be the reason that we decide to begin mindfulness practice, in the hope of learning a better way to cope.

Pain

Pain can arise from illness, such as fibromyalgia, but at other times we are not 'ill' as such; instead there is an injury, or physical tension. Back pain can, for example, make seated meditation nothing short of torture. It's easy to underestimate how debilitating and undermining chronic pain can be: there is the feeling that no one wants to hear about what you are going through, so you end up keeping it to yourself. There may be the option of pain relief, but the side effects of medication are sometimes almost as bad as the pain itself.

Sleepiness

Sometimes we don't realise that we're tired. We sit or lie down to practise, and suddenly all we want to do is sleep. In the body scan this is a particular problem, but it also happens in seated meditation. Sleep may be a form of aversion: *if I can just fall asleep, then I won't have to 'do' this meditation*; or it may be what we really need most at this moment.

Exhaustion

At one time or another in our lives, we all suffer from exhaustion. This is extreme tiredness, where we do not feel better after a night's sleep. The reasons for exhaustion are numerous: looking after a baby, too much work, studying late for exams, deadlines, worry, stress, ill health, insomnia, and so on. Whatever the cause, the result is the same: it's hard to get through the next day. There's no energy to enjoy life, no energy to look after ourselves. There is a strong tendency to reach for caffeine and 'quick fix' (sugary) foods, both of which end up making us feel more depleted.

Insomnia

The inability to sleep is a common problem. Sometimes pain prevents sleep, but more often, it is the mind which will not 'switch off'. Thoughts go round and round, gnawing away at something that happened earlier in the day which left us feeling uncomfortable – or going into fast forward, creating huge and disastrous scenarios about all the things that might go wrong tomorrow. It can seem that the moment our head hits the pillow, the brain shifts into overdrive. And once this pattern gets going, we experience the added anxiety about not being able to sleep: *if I can't get to sleep, tomorrow is going to be really awful*. This anxiety, of course, makes us even more wakeful, and can send us into 'fight or flight' mode, at which point sleep becomes a completely unobtainable goal.

Insomnia undermines our will and our enthusiasm, and therefore it can be a serious impediment to wanting to practise meditation. After all, mindfulness is about being *awake* to our experience: and if we are suffering with insomnia, what we most want is to be asleep.

Working with physical obstacles

When illness, pain or fatigue is present, our task is to figure out how to be with it. This is not an easy process: if we veer too far in the direction of strict discipline and a macho approach, we lose any sense of self-compassion. If we just give up attempting to practise because of minor discomfort, we miss out on vital opportunities to contact our inner stillness. In order to steer a steady course between these two extremes, the question we need to keep asking is: *How can I best look after myself at this moment?* Using that question as our guiding star, we can now look at some specific approaches to the obstacles that we face.

The mindful approach to tiredness

This is a good place to begin, as it's one we will all experience from time to time. Feeling sleepy may prevent us from beginning to practise, but it is more likely to arise once we have made an attempt to do some meditation. If you can notice sleepiness before you've actually fallen asleep, you're doing well! Here are some simple ways to work with sleepiness:

- Practise with your eyes open.
- Try looking up towards the ceiling for three seconds; this wakes up the attention.
- Take some deeper breaths.
- Introduce movement to the body. A short sequence of mindful stretching or yoga, particularly where you open up the breathing, will help you to stay awake once you move into meditation.
- Be aware that a meditation practice may actually make you feel more rested than trying to take a short nap.

- Let the sleepiness be your object of attention. Which parts of the body feel sleepy? Do any parts of the body feel awake?

- The traditional texts on the subject of sleepiness suggest rousing the mind by contemplating 'stirring objects'; namely, birth, decay, disease and death. This may sound a bit extreme, but the message is clear: our time on this earth is limited, so wake up!

- And do remember, if you are truly suffering with deep exhaustion, that the most skilful way to look after yourself may be to rest now, and practise later.

Using mindfulness with insomnia

If insomnia is a problem, the best place to intervene is *before* you go to bed. Here is a recipe that many people have found helpful:

- At some point in the day, try to get some fresh air and some sort of gentle exercise (walking is fine).

- Next, stop taking in caffeine after about 6 p.m. (And reduce the amount you have in the day.)

- One hour before bedtime, turn off the computer, the phone and the television.

- Change the lighting in the room – lighting a candle or two will create a different atmosphere.

- Next, practise some mindful yoga (if yoga doesn't suit you, choose a different practice) – a full forty minutes is useful. You need this amount of time to completely shift the mind and body and the breath out of 'doing' and into 'being'. (See pages 15–16 in Chapter 3, on the autonomic nervous system for more on this.) Keep bringing the mind back to the body, to the breath, to sensations.

- After yoga, take a hot bath or shower; it is the cooling-down process of the body after the bath that helps the body to sleep.
- Once you are in bed, use some simple words as you breathe in ... and out ... to anchor the mind in the present:

In ... Out

Deep ... Slow

Any time the mind wanders off, bring it back to these phrases.

Maintaining this regime retrains the body-mind to move into the present, and into a state of greater ease. From here, sleep is the natural result.

Illness and pain

Many people take up mindfulness practice because they are in physical pain. What's more, people who regularly practise mindfulness meditation say that it reduces the amount of pain they are in.

But mindfulness does not take away the pain.

So what is going on?

There is an old saying:

The wise person feels the pain of one arrow.

The unwise feels the pain of two. [1]

The first arrow is something that happens – perhaps I get a migraine, or flu. I probably can't avoid either of those, they just happen from time to time. And so the body will feel pain and discomfort.

And then there is what the mind does: the worry that I will not be able to manage my commitments, that I will be letting people down, that this pain will never end, that I can't bear it, etc. This mental activity is the second arrow: it is the suffering I create around the flu or the migraine. And the key is that I *have created it*. I have made up a narrative (I am letting people down) that makes me suffer more.

It's not just our minds that shoot the second arrow. Any time we are in physical pain, and particularly if the pain is chronic, our body tends to create its own 'second arrow'. In other words, we tense up. We start to protect the pain by holding that part of the body still, until we have built up muscular armour around the original site of pain. This rigidity carries its own pain, but most of the time we are unable to distinguish this secondary suffering from the original injury. It all just becomes a big bundle of pain, which in turn affects our mental and emotional well-being.

The mindful approach to pain

The common approach to pain is to either get rid of it (pain-killers, massage, etc.) or to distract ourselves from it (TV, the computer, social events). Both of these approaches have their usefulness. But the mindful approach is different. Mindfulness invites us to examine the pain; in other words, to become intimate with the sensation. Where is it? Can I describe it? Does it move? Are there replaces in the body without pain? Is it actually continuous, or are there moments without pain? How is it if I move or breathe in a certain way? Mindfulness involves letting go not only of the natural aversion that we have to pain, but also of the fear around it. Fear is part of the second arrow: *Is it always going to be this bad? What if it gets worse? How will I cope?*

Mindfulness invites us to invest all of our attention in just how things are at this moment. *This* is where the pain is now.

This is how it feels now. It takes considerable courage to turn towards the pain, but the rewards of doing so are enormous. In our willingness to become intimate with our pain, just as it is, we pull the second arrow from our flesh. This means that although the pain may still be present, the suffering that we have created around the pain has softened. And what is more wonderful: by moving into present-moment, non-judgmental awareness, we have taken an obstacle to practice (our pain) and turned it into the object of our practice. Simply by shifting our attitude, we have transformed our experience. This doesn't mean that you will enjoy being ill or in pain, but it does mean that you can create a sense of peace within the discomfort. Here is a story from Toni, who came to mindfulness because of physical pain:

> I booked to go on the introductory mindfulness course when I was four months into a bad bout of shingles. I was on a lot of drugs because of the intense pain. I had done the first three classes – and then one night at 2 a.m., I got up to go to the toilet and (perhaps because of the drugs) I missed the turning, fell down the stairs, and broke my neck.
>
> I arrived at the mindfulness class the next week with a neck collar: I couldn't do much, but meditating was very helpful. The idea of focusing on the pain rather than pushing it away: we had watched the Kabat-Zinn video with him describing this. It is totally counter-intuitive, but it really works. So in a way I learnt to befriend the pain. I looked for it, missed it when it is quiet, and longed for it to go as well. At that time, the pain defined who I was.
>
> After the broken neck, the doctor told me that I had to stop taking painkillers. At that point I think mindfulness became especially important. When I came off the drugs, the pain did not increase (nor lessen much at first) but it was not the catastrophe at all that I had thought it would be.

What mindfulness taught me, I think, is how to go towards the pain. When you do that, you achieve a kind of intimacy, where you are no longer so afraid, and where you are no longer fighting with your sensations. This enables you to relax, to feel the muscles that are holding you so tight begin to let go. It is *not* easy to do this, but knowing that it is possible really helped me get through a difficult time.

Toni's story demonstrates tremendous courage, especially in her willingness to stop struggling with her pain. As we learn to change our relationship to the pain, it actually has the potential to become a valuable ally. Through experiencing our own pain, we begin to have greater compassion for the suffering of those around us. Pain teaches us how to be patient. Pain teaches us about transience – that sensations come and go. While no one chooses to be in pain, the potential we have to befriend our experience enables us to become wiser and kinder in our relationship with the world.

7.
Attachments and desires

Silk threads revealed by the winter sun, horizontal,
glistening, holding the forest together.

Attachments form some of our deepest habitual patterns. These are the parts of our life that we think we must have in order to function; therefore, they are not easy to give up. Often we are attached to some view we have of how we want the future to be, because we believe it will make us happy or fulfilled. The problem with attachments is threefold. First, if we feel attached to something that we actually have, we can spend a lot of time and energy worrying that we will be miserable if we lose it. Second, if we are attached to the idea of getting something we do not already have, all of our energy drives us forward into the future and towards obtaining whatever it is we want – thus, we are never present. And third, wanting is a habit, or even an addiction. If we manage to get one thing, we tend to turn our habit of wanting towards getting the next thing, and the next, and the next. This means that in the end, no matter how successful we are at 'getting' the things we think we want, we are no longer able to be simply present and appreciate them.

In terms of practising mindfulness, the issue with attachments is that they are insistent: they convince us that we need to attend to them first, before we can do anything else. The following are various attachments that mindfulness students have encountered that interfere with getting down to practise.

The 'To Do' list

When we have many things to remember, having a list is incredibly useful. A 'To Do' list may be internal (the shopping list in our minds) or external (the bit of paper that reminds us of all the things we need to get done today). But the underlying message of such a list is that we cannot possibly stop until everything is ticked off, and often the list has more on it than we can manage in one day. So long as there are unfinished items on the list, the feeling may arise that we cannot – *we are not allowed to* – pause and take time to turn towards a mindfulness practice.

Time

The problem of time is one that everyone encounters. There is simply not enough time to do everything that we think we have to, or want to, do. Time drives us: we worry that we will late for the next appointment, moving into stress mode because of the two small hands on the face of our watch. Human beings have manufactured mechanisms that tell the precise time, and then we let them imprison us. The subconscious message of modern life is that we need to become more and more efficient with our time. Scientists have now worked out exercise regimes that only require three minutes three times a week! This means that we can rush into the gym, spend three minutes on the cycling machine, and then rush out again. Always, we are rushing to the next appointment. Always, we are missing our life.

Goals and targets

In modern culture, a huge amount is invested in achieving goals. As children we 'have to' pass exams. We need good marks to get to the next stage, and the next. Our minds are always reaching forward into the future: *I must do well at this, or tomorrow I will not be where I want to be.* And then when we arrive in that 'tomorrow' we barely notice it, because we are looking ahead to the next goal. Part of this arises from the primitive necessity to be the top primate. Only the alpha male mates with the females, so that only his genes are transmitted to the next generation. And while human beings' social organisation is more subtle than that of apes, we still have, lurking within us, the competitive streak that urges us to be 'best' and which makes us feel inadequate when we believe that we have not achieved enough. The problem with always pushing ourselves to pass the next exam, and the next one, is that we are never present. We never look at the moment and say, 'Right now, let me be here, just as I am.' Mindfulness practice will not stop you from having goals and ambitions, but it does invite you to have regular moments of 'time out' from driving yourself forward.

Making things better

We spend most of our lives trying to improve things. Partly this is a creative urge, and partly it arises from the tremendous intelligence that humans have always used to make life easier. From the invention of the wheel to the vacuum cleaner, the match to the smallpox vaccine, the human mind loves to solve a problem. And although in our individual lives we may not manage to create something revolutionary, our impulse is the same: *if I added some salt, would this soup taste better?* What underlies our fixing nature is the feeling that things are not quite okay as they are. This perpetual discontent means that we are always busy, always building or remodelling or adjusting. Our habit energy of fixing is so strong that when mindfulness suggests *being with things just as they are,* something deep within us cannot accept that this would be useful or even possible.

Appetites

In the traditional books on meditation, 'sensual desires' was listed as one of the main obstacles for monks.[1] Nothing much has changed in 2,000 years, except that now, in our consumer culture, there is a fairly common attitude that we are entitled to satisfy *immediately* whatever appetite arises. If we fancy ice cream, we go out and get some. The same may appear to be true for sex. In our societies, we have tended to lose focus on what would be beneficial for us, individually or as a whole. Instead, we just spend our time trying to get what we want, without paying much attention to how it might impact on anyone else. Appetites are essentially selfish, and it is our selfishness that is an issue when we come to mindfulness practice. This is because the understanding that arises through practice is such a fundamentally different one of 'self' in which 'selfishness' is undermined: I might really want some chocolate ice cream, but going out in the car to get it involves polluting the air that we all breathe. The cows that produce the cream are expelling vast amounts of methane gas into the air, increasing greenhouse gases and global warming. The people in the ice cream factory may be on a zero hours contract in freezing conditions. And then there are the farmers in Africa being paid a pittance for their cocoa. When I start to see the whole picture of 'chocolate ice cream', my appetite for its rich creamy sweetness is balanced by all of the ethical complications involved. Therefore, the self that wishes to satisfy sensual desires is going to resist a more mindful view – because if that arises, it may involve getting through the whole evening without any ice cream.

Being too connected

These days we have temptations that two millennia ago no one had even imagined. We have smartphones and tablets that go with us everywhere, at every moment of the day. People can ring us, text us, email us, Facebook us, and even tweet. What's more, we are expected to respond immediately. Anyone with teenage children will know that if you ask them to turn off their electronic devices for the duration of a meal, it is almost as if you have switched off their life support. Our phones, which now allow us to surf the net and navigate, have become such a serious addiction that turning them off in order to sleep at night is, for some, genuinely challenging.

Here is a frightening fact: *in order to undertake mindfulness practice, you are going to have to switch off your phone.* To become connected to the real, three-dimensional world around you – the trees and the birds and the sky and the wind and your own breath – you are going to have to disconnect yourself from the virtual world of your two-dimensional screen. In a mindfulness class, the only real 'rule' is that people switch off their phones. For many people on the course, it will be the first time all day that they have become disconnected from their virtual network and not instantly available. Once they get over the initial uncertainty, being disconnected from the virtual world and beginning to reconnect with simply being here and now is an unexpected pleasure, and a genuine letting go into a state of greater ease.

The mindful approach to attachments

Each one of us has our own special attachments. Therefore, the place to begin is, as always, with noticing. There are certain parts of our life, such as food and sleep, that we really do need in order to be well. But there may be other things that we imagine we need or want – and this imagining creates suffering. It's worth taking some time to reflect on this, and possibly to make a list of what you feel you cannot do without.

One fascinating aspect of attachments and desires is that most of them seem to pull us towards the future. We are attempting to gain something (house, job, partner, happiness) that we lack at this moment. What we have now is not sufficient; we believe that we will only be satisfied when we get some certain thing, at some point in the future. No doubt you have had this experience: you finally get the object or the situation you have craved, only to face another wave of feeling that it is not enough. There is no end to striving.

Now, take a moment to let your mind move into the future in a different way. Imagine yourself when you are nearing the end of your life. As you look back over all that you have done and achieved, what is really important to you? Is it a pair of shoes you bought, or a car? Is it your appearance, or how much money you have made? Or is it the quality of your relationships, the moments when someone was kind to you, the times you were genuinely present for your loved ones? Being in touch with what we truly value and understanding what actually makes us happy are useful guides in helping us let go of things that we might not genuinely need. The less attached we are to material objects, the less time and money we will spend in this way. This frees up time and energy to use in other ways – in ways that nourish and sustain us on a deeper level.

Ultimately, in order to unhook ourselves from the pattern of chasing after more and more, we simply need to turn the attention to the present; and in doing so, to begin to appreciate all that we have around us. In this turning towards what is, rather than to a fantasy of the future, we can begin to realise that we need surprisingly little in order to be well and happy.

Here is another wonderful secret: happiness does not arise through gaining, it arises through being present. Once we understand this, so much of the suffering that we experience – from the feeling that there is too much to do, that there is not enough time, and so on – lessens dramatically. This does not mean that we stop having responsibilities and dreams, but it does mean we can learn to hold them more lightly, just as Rumi's poem 'Who Makes These Changes?' suggests:

> Who makes these changes?
> I shoot an arrow right.
> It lands left.
> I ride after a deer and find myself
> Chased by a hog.
> I plot to get what I want
> And end up in prison.
> I dig pits to trap others
> And fall in.
>
> I should be suspicious
> Of what I want.[2]

Creating a new relationship with time

The common view of time (there isn't enough of it) is certainly an obstacle to practice. However, through practising mindfulness, a different relationship to time is allowed to develop. At first, we begin to notice that time is elastic. A few moments, if we are enjoying the sensations of breathing, can feel like a vast oasis that changes the whole rest of the day. On the other hand, if we are in pain, thirty minutes can feel like an eternity. Time is different each time we practise – and this difference comes down to our mental state. With aversion, time seems to be moving too slowly (oh when is this going to be over?). If we are doing something we really enjoy, time may well seem to be slipping away too fast – because we want the enjoyable experience to go on and on.

In fact, when we are truly present, we discover that there is no time. We are just here. The present moment, when we allow ourselves to experience it fully, has the feeling that the clocks have ceased to exist. In fact, it is not a moment at all: it is a spacious, timeless, open field. As the spiritual teacher Krishnamurti said, 'To meditate is to be innocent of time.'[3]

And so, at some point, once you have some confidence in how to practise mindful meditation, allow yourself this radical experiment: take off the watch, turn off the phone, and sit down to meditate – without a recorded practice or a clock to guide you. Sit down in the present and allow your experience to unfold without any pressure from the construct of 'time'. Don't worry about how long you sit: time simply doesn't come into it. Sit until there arises a sense that the practice is complete. Let go of wondering how long the meditation was – time is an unnecessary fabrication, like wanting to put legs on a snake. Afterwards, allow yourself a cup of tea and perhaps a view of nature. There is nothing to hurry towards, and nothing else that you need.

8.
Aversion

Empty branches, brown sedge – nothing moves through this winter air – not even birdsong.

The hurdles listed in this chapter are the various ways in which we seek to avoid mindfulness practice, or indeed anything in our lives that we want to turn away from. Aversion has many subtle ways of presenting itself, sometimes masquerading as something else entirely.

Restlessness

Restlessness is a wonderfully effective form of avoidance. If the physical body is jumpy or agitated, it's really difficult to practise the body scan or seated meditation. Generally restlessness arises initially, at the start of a practice period, and tends to calm down as we sink into the practice. But at other times it can suddenly become overpowering after fifteen or twenty minutes, so that we feel we *have* to stop and get up and move around. Partly this is habit energy: the body is not accustomed to prolonged stillness while we are awake. Partly it is mental restlessness: something comes up in the mind from our 'To Do' list, and it suddenly seems to be vital that we do it right now – again, this is habit energy. On a deeper level, something within us resists letting go of 'doing': we can sense that as we go more deeply into practice, we may begin to move into a state of 'being'. Because this is unfamiliar territory, and beyond the control of the 'doing' mind, it often creates rest-lessness as a strategy in order to regain control. Restlessness is an escape route, and we need to see it for what it is – as a form of aversion – in order to know how to work with it wisely.

Boredom

Boredom is a common excuse. How often do children say this about something at school? If something is boring, then why bother to engage? Boredom is a way of 'zoning out', of not making an effort to understand. It is also a defence when we fear that we cannot understand. Instead of saying, 'I didn't understand that maths lesson', we can say, 'that was boring'. This way the onus is not on us – we are placing the fault on an external factor (the maths lesson) rather than on ourselves.

In mindfulness practice, boredom arises for everyone. It's incredibly reassuring to realise this. Learning how to work with boredom is actually part of practising. It is nearly always a sign that, in our practice, we need to dig deeper. This means that, while listening to the body scan, it is not enough to hear the instructions *(and now, just feeling the breath, coming into the body, and leaving the body).* Instead, we need to move into the realm of genuinely experiencing the breath – this breath, just as it is, right now. This requires a certain attitude and a certain kind of effort. Boredom is a signpost that something is not quite right with the effort that we are using.

Fear

Fear is what often lies beneath the veneer of boredom or rest-lessness. We may avoid practising because we are worried about what might come up when we stop and tune into the present. This is common when something has been suppressed – when our strategy for coping has been to avoid looking at whatever event or emotion we find difficult. Combining mindfulness with suppression is like trying to mix oil and water: it does not work. Mindful attention invites us to be present with whatever is arising, and in meditation, eventually pretty much everything in our psyche will bubble up to the surface. We cannot really pick and choose what we are willing to allow into the light of our awareness and what we are not. We need to be willing to be with whatever appears, even though it may be scary. Therefore, as long as there are aspects of your life that you are determined to avoid, practice is going to feel threatening. Here is a story to illustrate this problem.

Once there was a course participant who, shortly after signing up for the mindfulness course, was diagnosed with a serious illness. The illness produced physical sensations, and each time she practised the body scan, her awareness of these sensations was heightened. Because she was in the early stages of dealing with the diagnosis, her impulse was to ignore it as much as possible – but when she practised, ignoring it was not possible. And awareness of the sensations would lead her mind down the path of thinking about how the illness would develop, and how she would become less and less able to live an independent life. Feelings of anger and how unfair it was would follow close behind. So practising put her in touch with physical and psychological states that she was not ready to accept.

Mindfulness asks that we be with things just as they are, but when those things involve pain, anger and fear, it is easy to understand how distraction and denial might look like preferable options. For this particular student, the timing of the course was not right. In the long run, however, the more we try to avoid our pain, the more narrow, anxious and exhausting our life becomes. Turning towards distress is not easy, but it does ultimately offer a path of greater ease, as the following story from Ali explains:

> I went on a mindfulness course because of anxiety. I was under a lot of pressure at work, and I'd got to the point where everything was making me feel more and more anxious. I was even having panic attacks.
>
> What happened, when I started to meditate, is that I became more aware of how I was feeling – the terrible physical feelings of anxiety – so it was like everything actually got worse. I am not sure how I managed to carry on, but what I discovered was, if I just kept sitting for the whole of the thirty minutes, by the end I felt calmer. It was like at first the volume of the anxiety got turned up, and then it got turned down. It was a kind of process. Once I understood this process, I got more willing to sit with the strong feelings that came up – because I knew that they would pass, and that I would start to feel better.

Ali's experience offers us an important lesson: mindfulness involves allowing difficult emotions to be present. Ali stopped trying to avoid the anxiety, and instead began to accept it. If we can find the courage to be with this process, whatever arises begins to disperse. In overcoming the fear that we feel, we begin to liberate thoughts and emotions that we imagined were too difficult. Mindfulness enables us to do this in a gentle way, one breath at a time, knowing that we have our foundation of being present in each moment to keep us stable and safe.

Fear that things will fall apart

There are times in our lives when we are only just managing – when it feels as though we are juggling several balls in the air, worried that if we pause for even a moment, everything will come crashing down around us. In the midst of this complicated juggling act, taking time out to practise mindfulness can appear to be a risky strategy: *if I stop – or even pause – the whole world around me might grind to a halt.* This is a particularly dangerous possibility if we dislike some of those balls that we have been continuously juggling (perhaps the 'work' one). *If I stop, will I actually be able to make myself start again?* There is a real danger of wanting to walk away and leave some of the balls lying on the ground.

Part of the problem here is the desire to feel less stressed, combined with the view that we dare not make any changes. And through mindfulness practice, there will be changes. It is inevitable, when we truly begin to notice our lives and how we inhabit them, that our appreciation, our relationships, our priorities, will evolve.

Mindfulness is, in part, a process of befriending ourselves: of beginning to appreciate and listen to our inner voice. So often that voice is drowned out by all of the busy-ness going on around us and within us. In developing the courage to sit quietly with ourselves, it is possible that we begin to notice some aspects of the way we live that do not offer ourselves or the world any benefit. Once again, we need to find courage to be with this awareness, and the discomfort it brings, without turning away or ignoring it, as the next story shows.

This student described herself as a 'lady who lunches' and indeed, for many years, she did. Then her husband had a heart attack, and she was left caring for him, as well as suddenly having to go back to work to support the family. She spoke fast, she walked fast, she did everything in a hurry, and could barely sleep, simply because she was trying to cope with feeling that all of the family responsibility was now on her shoulders. Imagine how difficult it was for her to turn off her phone, not to mention practising the body scan! At the end of the mindfulness course, in reflecting how mindful practice had impacted on her life she said, simply, 'I learnt to stop.'

Impatience

Allied to juggling is the sense of hurry. *How can I sit here for thirty minutes when there is so much to do?* Impatience, or hurry, is a strong form of habit energy. It pushes us to eat quickly, drive quickly, text quickly. It means that we are always in a rush to get on to the next thing, which in turn means that we are never actually present. Being truly present, in an open and timeless way, is the antidote to hurry, but it is medicine that many of us, because we are so driven, find difficult to swallow. Hurry can make us feel important and give us a buzzy, adrenalin-fuelled energy that is deeply seductive. But being hurried and busy can become an end in itself rather than a means to actually achieving anything worthwhile.

Rebelliousness

Everyone, at one time or another, has experienced someone in power who forces us do something that seems unreasonable. Perhaps it was a teacher, a parent, a boss. Perhaps we were punished for something we did not do. Perhaps the authority figure was stressed out, and took it out on us in some way. This experience can leave us with the feeling that *we don't like being told what to do*. A teacher might suggest doing something we would normally enjoy, but because it feels like we are being ordered to do it, we don't want to. We resist. We rebel.

Rebellion is sometimes necessary. Rising up against political tyranny, or blowing the whistle when we see others being abused – we have, at times, a moral imperative to rebel against the status quo. But, like any other aspect of our nature, it can become habitual. We can be suspicious and resistant of what someone asks us to do, even when we know that it might be in our best interests.

The mindful approach to aversion

Begin by noticing the fact that aversion is present. Judgments may accompany the 'not wanting to' – things such as, 'I shouldn't be feeling this way', or 'I hate feeling restless and bored' (aversion about aversion). Look deeply, and see if there is something beneath the surface of the aversion. Fear may be lurking beneath restlessness; anger and irritation may be somewhere within boredom. Whatever you discover, this is just how it is right now. Remember, one of the great gifts of mindfulness is that we focus on *what is*.

However, once we have identified the specifics of our aversion, it is not wise simply to continue to dwell on it. Instead, we need to find a skilful way of responding to the negativity, so that we can begin to look after ourselves. The point is, if aversion is rising within us, we are suffering. Dislike, ill will, suspicion, hatred – all of these are forms of internal poison. Once we realise this, it becomes obvious that we need special care. One of the most skilful ways to respond to these poisons is with the practice of kindness meditation.

Kindness meditation

Kindness meditation, or *metta bhavana* as it is called in Pali, is the cultivation of friendliness.[1] This can involve directing the friendliness towards others, but when we are experiencing aversion, we need to begin by offering friendliness towards ourselves. If our mental habit energy is negative and aversive, then it is likely that at least some of this gets directed at ourselves: in fact, people often find it difficult to wish themselves well. If this is the case for you, then you are certainly prey to the energy of ill will and aversion. The important point here is that, having mindfully observed the unhelpful habit energy of the mind, it is then important to find a way of acting skilfully, so that we are not stuck in a self-critical rut.

Kindness practice is more than 2,500 years old. Traditionally it uses phrases that the practitioner repeats in his or her mind. There are different possible phrases, such as:

> *May I be safe and well.*
>
> *May I be free from suffering.*
>
> *May I live with joy and ease.*

Pause, and read these words over again. Take your time. Try it again.

It doesn't matter if you feel you 'deserve' to be free from suffering, or if you feel you will never be completely well, or if joy feels like an emotion completely out of reach. It only matters that you repeat the words in your mind.

What is happening when we practise kindness towards ourselves is that we are thinking a different kind of thought. To explain this, here is a useful analogy:

Let's imagine that I need to go see a friend who lives on the other side of a large wheatfield. I walk through the wheat, beating down a path, until I arrive at her house. Now let's say that the next day comes, and I want to make the journey again. I will walk on the same path, because it is easier to walk on the path that I've already made, rather than to trample down a new one. Well, it turns out that our brains are a bit like the wheatfield: the first time we think a thought (*may I be well*) it takes some effort, because we haven't thought it before. But as we repeat the thought, it becomes easier. It's the same when we learn a language: at first it's difficult to remember how to ask for a cup of tea, but the more we do it, the more confidence we have, and the easier it gets, until it feels natural.

In the brain, the neural pathways of thoughts that we think over and over (no matter whether it's 'may I be well' or 'I'm a worthless human being') become like super-highways: the thoughts travel more and more easily the more we go down that mental path.

Therefore, in the kindness practice, we are creating a new pathway through the brain. We are replacing a negative thought (*this meditation is boring*) with a different thought (*may I live with joy and ease*). Repetition embeds this new way of thinking. With aversive thinking, just dwelling on how much we don't like something is not helpful. And so here is another key secret in the practice of working with aversion: we may need to take the skilful decision to change the pathway we are treading – both in our minds and in our lives.

For more on kindness practice, see page 100 in Chapter 15 on 'The toolkit'.

9.
Depression

This morning, on the way to the hut, noticing something in the undergrowth – a shape, a colour, like a bit of old clothing. Then realising that it is a fox, the fox who lives here in the garden. His body is lifeless, and one of his ears has been chewed. In the summer months, we shared the garden, me sitting in the shade and him in the sun, only a few metres apart. He became so accustomed to my human presence that, as I sat, he would sleep. I could tell if he was about from his smell – and probably he recognised me in the same way. We knew each other, in that strange, magical way that one can know a wild creature. And now, he is gone.

Depression is what motivates many people to begin mindfulness, as a way of preventing relapse. But it is also an obstacle, because if we're feeling depressed, we lack the motivation to actually practise.

Depression is complicated. In fact, it's so complicated that it's difficult to know exactly how to categorise it. It certainly involves aversion, but it is more than a low emotional state. It also produces unskilful views (see Chapter 10) but it is more than the negative thoughts we have towards ourselves. Depression is physiological (low serotonin in the brain) and often there is a genetic predisposition. It affects our bodies – the lethargy that depression induces is certainly physical as well as mental. The sense of hopelessness and despair can feel as though it's infecting every cell in the body. Depression can arise after a shock or trauma or lack of sunlight, but it can also arise for no clear reason at all. Most of us will feel depressed at one time or another, so perhaps it is as normal a human experience as joy or anger or hunger. But the problem with depression is that, for some, it becomes so incapacitating that normal life grinds to a halt for weeks or even months. And worse than that, if you have been depressed once, the chances are that it will visit you again.

Perhaps here it would be useful to define depression. Doctors say that you are depressed if you have five or more of the following symptoms for at least two weeks:

- Feeling depressed or sad most of the day
- Less interested in and taking less pleasure from normal daily activities
- Weight loss or weight gain; or increased/decreased appetite
- Difficulty sleeping at night, or sleeping more in the day
- Feeling 'slowed down' or agitated during the day
- Feelings of worthlessness, or overwhelming guilt
- Difficulties concentrating or thinking; indecisiveness
- Recurring thoughts of suicide or death[1]

Research indicates that mindfulness practice is at least as useful as drugs for preventing a relapse of depression, as long as you have already suffered three or more bouts. This raises an interesting question: why do you need to have experienced at least three depressive phases in order for mindfulness to be useful? This question may be answered by the following diagram of a spiral.

Figure 1. Life's spiral and experiences of depression

As you look at this diagram, imagine that the spiral represents your life as it moves outwards from the centre (your earliest experiences, or your genetic inheritance). Periodically in your life, you meet the straight line. If you imagine that the straight line represents a depressive streak, then every time your spiral meets that line, you experience depression. But each time, because the spiral is expanding, your perspective on the depressive episode changes; in other words, you develop a broader view. Over time you become familiar with it: you know the signs, and you know that it is episodic. But if you have only experienced depression once, you simply do not have this view. The same is true for any condition that comes and goes: our understanding of it and our relationship to it changes each time we meet it.

When to do a mindfulness course

If you suffer from depression, and you would like to try mindfulness, one of the dilemmas you may face is when to start. Taking on something new if you are in the depths of despond is not possible: if it's difficult to get out of bed, it's unreasonable to expect that you should start going to a new class, or have the energy to begin meditation. Therefore, with depression, there is a 'catch 22' situation: it might well do you good, but you are not up to doing it. If depression is a recurrent visitor in your life, you need to somehow arrange a mindfulness course at a time when you are not at your lowest ebb.

But what if you've been practising for a while, and then depression threatens to return? This is when, as mindfulness practitioners, we need to summon our greatest skill and wisdom. First, it's vital to recognise the symptoms. If we have flu, we recognise it through the fever and the aches and pains. With depression, the symptoms are often thoughts: *mindfulness is just another thing I've failed at,* or *I'm so worthless that not even meditation can help me,* are possible symptoms of depression. They are not true or helpful or pleasant. They are just symptoms. The other major symptom that accompanies depression is the loss of motivation. *What's the use in getting out of bed to meditate? It's all pointless, isn't it?* Once again, it's vital to see this view as a symptom rather than as reality. Usually, when we are in a good state, we feel motivated to do something, and so we do it. But when we are depressed, this approach doesn't work. Instead, we need to coax ourselves to try some small practice even though we don't much feel like it. Once we've taken the first step, a bit of energy arises, and we realise that we feel better. This realisation helps us to do a bit more. In depression, the action has to come first, and then the motivation grows out of this first effortful action.

One of the common features of people who suffer from depression is that they have high expectations of themselves. If they are going to practise, then it had better be a full practice – no half measures are acceptable. Clearly, these high expectations are themselves an obstacle when energy and motivation are lacking. The secret to working with unrealistic expectations is, first, to notice that that they have arisen. In the act of noticing our habit energy, we can begin to unstick ourselves from it, by questioning its assumptions. *Perhaps, for instance, it would actually be enough right now, given the way I am feeling, to just lie down and feel my breath for a minute or two.* In the willingness to contemplate gentler alternatives, we are cultivating kindness towards ourselves, and it is this kindness that will enable us to come up with an approach that is manageable and nourishing.

The good news, when we are feeling depressed, is that even a small action can have a significant impact on our mood and our view. Here are some suggestions for ways to practise when depressed. Please don't feel that you need to do them all – just choose one that sounds realistic.

> ➤ Bringing awareness to the next three breaths. You are already breathing, so this only requires a shift in attention. In paying attention to the breath, you are letting go of the ruminative mind.

> ➤ Lying on your back, on the floor, with the knees bent and the soles of the feet on the ground, in a way that feels comfortable. Place your hands on the abdomen, and notice the breath. Carry on for five breaths, or ten. Once you have done this, listen to the body: is there a simple stretch that it would appreciate? Perhaps experiment with lifting the arms up over your head as you breathe in, and back down to the ground as you breathe out.

> Going for a mindful walk outside. It doesn't need to be a long walk; you can just go to the end of the garden, or the street. Notice the world, and how the air feels on the skin, and your posture. If you can, walk directly on the earth – not on concrete or asphalt. Being in touch with the earth can be deeply healing. Knowing that you are connecting with the earth, and feeling how it supports you, can be a wonderful gift when times are difficult.

> Appreciating. No matter where you are, no matter how awful the circumstances, there will be something that, if you search for it, you will find that you can appreciate. Perhaps the sunlight, or a flower, or some music. Perhaps your own inhalation. Perhaps your hands, that are allowing you to hold this book, or your eyes, that enable you to see. Learning how to appreciate small things in our lives can transform the energy in our minds and hearts.

> Smiling. This is a challenging practice for anyone in depression, but smiling changes our facial muscles, and our mood. Because our ability to enjoy things is diminished when we feel depressed, it takes effort to find something that can make us smile. Perhaps it is birdsong, or a plant, or a photograph of someone we love. Turning towards something joyful helps to overcome the habit energy of just focusing on the negative aspects of our life.

> Labelling your thoughts. If you are feeling worthless, notice that this is just a judging thought. If the mind is going over some past action, notice that this is remembering. By tuning into the habit energy of the mind, the thoughts begin to lose their power.

Remember this: thoughts are not facts, they are just transitory fabrications on the pathways of the brain. And we can choose to take a different pathway, just by being aware. (For more on labelling thoughts, see pages 109–111.)

Here is Sally's story about depression and practice:

For many years, as a teenager and into my twenties, I was depressed. It was like a constantly dark grey sky: I went to work and mostly functioned, but I never felt even a bit happy. It went on and on, year after year after year. Then one day I found a book about meditation, and I started to practise – I can't even remember why ... but something about it made sense to me. At more or less the same time, I started yoga. I wasn't doing either of these things to 'cure' depression, because I don't think I even had any idea that it was possible to feel any different. But within a few months, I felt different. Instead of feeling like existence was a miserable burden, I started to appreciate the world. I started to feel grateful. In fact, everything changed. I actually started to enjoy being alive.

Sally's words remind us that our experience does always change – which is easy to forget in the midst of a depressed phase. Knowing that our mood is transient (remember the image of the spiral) is actually a key factor in managing to avoid being overwhelmed by the dark clouds. Behind those dark clouds, there is sunshine. We just need to keep looking after ourselves, with kindness, until the sun breaks through.

10.
Unhelpful views

Droplets on this leaf; in the intimacy of fog, distance vanishes.

Some unhelpful views are variations on the theme of aversion, but because people mention them frequently when reflecting on obstacles to mindful practice, they warrant their own special section. Perhaps the most common of these unhelpful views, and the most challenging, are those directed at ourselves. Here are some examples:

- I'm not any good at mindfulness
- What are other people going to think of me?
- I must be doing it wrong
- I should practise every day
- It's self-indulgent to take time to practise
- My mind is hopeless – it wanders all the time
- I already know how to be mindful

And then there are the unhelpful views we create around practice:

- I'm disappointed with how it's going
- I'm not sure it's going to help me (doubt)
- I can't see any results
- It all seems pointless

• I don't really need mindfulness right now

What all of these views share is that they are judgments. Either we are judging ourselves, and our failure to practise diligently enough, or we are judging the practice itself. Judging is one of the most fundamental functions in the human mind: it helps us to sort out what is useful from what is not. We judge a situation to be safe, or to be risky. We judge a particular food to be good for us, or not. Judging is a way of evaluating, which enables us to make choices about what we do each day. For example, without having made some sort of judgment about mindfulness and the problems you face in trying to practise it, you would not be reading this book.

Why then is an essential part of mindfulness about being non-judgmental? If judgments are useful and necessary, why are we asked to drop them?

The first difficulty with the judgments we make is that they are part of our habit energy. We make them so quickly, so automatically, that we barely know what is happening. If we make a positive judgment (I like *that*) then we react by trying to get whatever *that* is. If we make a negative judgment, we move into avoidance. Liking and disliking are intrinsically forms of black and white thinking: this is good, that is bad. There is no middle ground. And once we have made the judgment, we are no longer open to the subtleties of what we are judging. We have put it in a pigeonhole, and now we ignore it. In other words, judging is a way of shutting down. Once you have made a judgment, you are no longer open and curious.

The second issue with judgments is that we *believe* them. Once we have made a judgment, we honestly think that this is the way it is. No matter how much evidence arises to the contrary, it's likely that we will maintain our original view. So once the judgment is formed in the mind that 'I'm no good at mindfulness', then we truly believe that. We will notice all of the evidence that reinforces this view, and disregard any contradictory information. This is the real problem with unhelpful views – not that they arise, but that we believe in them. As the ancient philosopher Epictetus said: 'Men are not bothered by things, but by the view they take of them.'[1]

However, by turning the light of mindfulness onto our judgments, suddenly we create a choice: *Is this really how it is? ... perhaps I am not so sure.* Seung Sahn, the Zen Master who taught Jon Kabat-Zinn in America, used to sign every letter 'Only Don't Know'.[2] *Only don't know* is a wonderful way to approach life – because, truly, we don't know. We never see the whole picture, we never know the beginning of the story, or its end. By recognising that we don't know, our judgments dissolve, to be replaced by curiosity. Freed from the tyranny of judging, we can begin to appreciate the joy that arises when we look at our world with fresh eyes.

The Third Secret

Understanding the Roots of Resistance

11.
Working with resistance: the first key

The smell of the wood smoke offers up a primitive, ancestral sense of being settled here, of being home.

The inner path

We lead busy lives. Because we are busy, we get stressed. Because we are stressed, we take up mindfulness. And then we have the problem of where to fit it in. One of the common approaches is that mindfulness practice becomes yet another item on our 'To Do' list:

- answer emails
- meeting with colleague
- tax return
- laundry
- cook supper
- meditation

If you look at this list, you can see how easy it is not to get around to 'meditation'. After all, we'll be fined if our tax return is late, and we all know we need clean underwear and food. The problem here is that meditation does not belong on the 'To Do' list. In a list of practical obligations, it is the odd one out.

To explain this, here is a story:

Plum Village is a large retreat centre in the south of France, which practises according to the teachings of the Vietnamese Zen Master, Thich Nhat Hanh. On one of their summer retreats, a monastic was telling a group of students about her outer path, and her inner one. Her outer path, she said, was one of service. She helped to organise the huge retreats there, with hundreds of participants. Food, accommodation, work parties: from 5 a.m. to 10 p.m., she and all of the other monastics worked tirelessly to make a good retreat for everyone there (including dozens of children). No doubt, they had a lot of 'To Do' lists.

But, as she explained, she also had an inner path. Her inner path was one of meditation, awareness, reflection, creativity. Her inner path put her in touch with nature as she walked through the plum orchards. Without being in touch with her inner path, it was not possible to successfully maintain her outer path. The inner path was the foundation on which the outer path could be built.

Here is the crucial point of this story: her inner path was not merely another item on the 'To Do' list of her outer path. Her inner path existed on an entirely different level, springing up from a place deep within her; and only because she nourished it was she able to accomplish the demanding outer path of looking after everyone else.

We, every one of us, are the same. We have the outer path: the laundry, the meals, work, etc. But we also have an inner path. For many of us, this path is so rarely used that it is overgrown and seemingly impenetrable. This is why mindfulness practice can feel daunting at first. Somewhere deep within us we all have a sense that our inner path exists, but clearing it and keeping back the weeds so that we can use it may feel like too huge a task – especially when the outer path is overwhelming us.

Therefore, to take even one step on this path requires that we turn towards a deeper part of our being. We need to recognise that our inner path exists, and that we actually want to explore it. Practising mindful meditation, we begin to be more aware of this inner path. And the more aware we are of the inner path, the easier it is to practise.

But how to begin to contact this inner path?
Remember the question from Chapter 4?
Here it is again:

What is your deepest wish?

Reflect on this. Each time you approach the question, something new may bubble up. Each answer that arises is like the needle on your very own compass: and that needle is pointing directly towards your inner path.

12.
Working with resistance: the second key

Now, standing by the small stream that runs through this woodland. The water is clear, chattering, fast moving, creating a dance of lines and patterns as it negotiates each stone. On the map this stream has a name, as if it were a fixed thing. But nothing about it, not even its channel, is fixed. The water droplets that pass by now may never have been here before, and may never happen this way again. At each second, the stream is entirely new, an endless rhythm of movement and transience. Standing still, witnessing the continual flow and song of the stream, and realising that we are no different. We seem solid, but we are not. Thoughts and feelings and cells – they catch the light for a moment, and then they move on.

The foundation of most of the kinds of resistance we encounter is something so elusive that we often fail to see it: our own self. Or it might be better to describe it as our notion of our self – who we think we are. This picture we have – our internal 'selfie' – is the story we hold in our minds of 'me'. This 'me' has a history, it has reasons from childhood for 'my' behaviour. It has fears. It has a long list of things it needs in order that 'I' may feel happy and fulfilled. This selfie is a fabricated and fixed view: it is the narrative we believe in, in which 'I' am an individual, and the hero or the heroine of 'my' story, with the universe revolving around 'me'.

But, if you begin to look deeply, you will begin to see the notion we have of ourselves as separate and individual is not quite right. In order to understand this, take a moment and feel this page in your hand. If you are lucky enough to be holding a real book, feel the texture of the paper, its thickness, its colour. Now pause, and consider where this paper came from. It came from a tree. Think about how that tree grew. It needed rain that fell from clouds, and air and earth, and all of the organisms in the earth that helped give life to the tree. If you really appreciate this page fully, you will see that it is made up of many elements – tree, water, earth, air – and that it could not exist without them. In other words, this piece of paper does not have a separate, independent existence. It is related to, and exists because of, many other factors. We may not usually look up at a cloud and think, 'That cloud is in this book', but actually, if we look more deeply, we see that it is. The same is true of everything around us, and even ourselves. We, as human beings, only exist because of our ancestors, and the earth which produces our food, and the water in our rivers that we drink, and the air that we breathe. Our existence cannot actually be separated from any of these elements – we need all of them to support our life. So when we look at the palm of our hand, if we really look, we see our family tree, and also the whole earth. We are dependent upon, and completely made up of, elements which are apparently 'not me'. Therefore, the notion that we have of being separated from the rest is, as Albert Einstein said, 'A kind of optical delusion of our consciousness.'[1]

The historical and the ultimate dimensions

Each one of us grew up in a particular place, with a particular group of people, and with particular gifts and difficulties. We are each part of a cultural paradigm that influences our view of ourselves and the world. This is what the Vietnamese Zen Master Thich Nhat Hanh calls 'the historical dimension'. The only problem with this historical dimension is that we tend to invest in it so completely that we fail to realise it is not our whole existence. There is another, larger dimension which we inhabit: Thich Nhat Hanh calls this 'the ultimate dimension'.[2]

The ultimate dimension holds the historical 'story of me' dimension within it, but it is an infinitely broader view, containing the whole of existence within this timeless moment of being. A helpful analogy is this: think about the surface of the sea. The waves rise up, each one appearing to have an individual existence, and then they fall back below the surface. In the historical dimension, they have a beginning, a time span of existence, and then they end. But the ultimate dimension is the whole sea, the whole body of water. When the little wave rises up, it is water. When it falls back below the surface of the sea, it is still water. It never stops being water. In this dimension, it has no beginning, and also no end. Its visible form changes: sometimes we can see it, and other times it is hidden, but it never loses its essential nature, which is water.

We also exist in the ultimate dimension, even though most of the time we are not aware of it. Most of the time, we are caught by our stories and plans, all of which are part of our historical, linear dimension. What happens, when we practise meditation, is that we begin to glimpse this other, deeper aspect of being. We move from our thinking mind (our 'selfie') to a more open awareness. We become a bigger container.[3] Our 'selfing' still goes on, but we can now hold it within a broader view – the view of awareness. From this perspective, the selfie that we have constructed is no longer the whole picture. Here we inhabit a different way of being – an experiential mode, in which we appreciate the genuine reality of how it feels at this moment to be alive. In this way, we begin to touch the ultimate dimension of existence. In other words, we realise that we are not mere individual waves of human existence: we are actually always part of the whole sea, as shown in Figure 2.

Figure 2. The historical and the ultimate dimensions

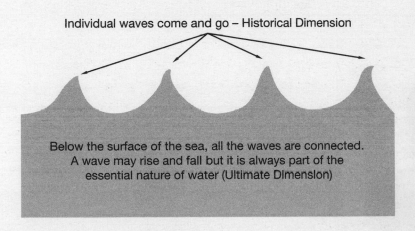

Individual waves come and go – Historical Dimension

Below the surface of the sea, all the waves are connected. A wave may rise and fall but it is always part of the essential nature of water (Ultimate Dimension)

Why is this broader view often difficult to embrace? Because our ego, our selfie self, likes to be the most important character in the room. It wants to be centre stage. It wants to be in control of our thoughts and our actions. It is like the toddler who won't let his mother speak to anyone else without throwing a tantrum. And being more subtle and skilful than a toddler (but no less demanding) it fabricates problems: fears, busy-ness, doubt, lethargy – in fact anything that might blow us off course and make it hard for us to practise.

Therefore, whenever an obstacle arises that is preventing you from practice, look deeper and notice if selfing is at work. There is no need to judge, no need to make 'should' statements around selfing – it is enough to notice what is happening. Selfing is rather like that scene in *The Wizard of Oz* where the wizard is creating a huge and frightening visual display for Dorothy and her friends. But Dorothy's little dog draws back the curtain, and the real wizard, an ordinary man, is revealed. Once the reality is known, we can accept our selfing, while at the same time appreciating the bigger picture, the deeper dimension that connects us to the whole world.

The Fourth Secret

Understanding How to Practise

13.
Three essentials

This morning the world is transformed – by snow. Bobble hats of white perch on top of the feeders. The female pheasants, normally so well camouflaged in their brown feathers, stand out against the white ground: and they seem to realise this, the way they tilt their heads sideways, constantly looking up into the sky with one eye, scouting for predators.

Many years ago a friend told me this. She had learnt it from a meditation teacher,[1] who in turn had probably learnt it from her own teacher. It is this: in order to practise meditation, you need to be able to accomplish three things:

1. keep a schedule
2. bow to your anger
3. limit the sphere of your activity

It sounds so simple, and yet, contained within these three simple requirements is a lifetime's work.

Keeping a schedule

This means that, if you decide that you are going to get up at 7 a.m. to practise mindful meditation, then you actually do it. Notice that it does not prescribe any particular schedule: you might decide to practise at 4 p.m., or 11 a.m., or midnight. The timing does not matter – what matters is that whatever time you allocate for practice, you stop everything else at that moment and turn your attention to practice.

In order for this to be possible, you need to set yourself a realistic schedule. There is no point deciding to meditate at 4 a.m. if you know you can't make yourself get out of bed then.

Also, if you do shift work, then your meditation schedule needs to alter according to your work schedule. If your child has a fever, you can't suddenly leave him or her at 8 p.m. to practise sitting meditation. But you can practise while you are sitting together, both of you breathing in and out. So the schedule is a structure, rather than a straightjacket. Use it wisely, and it will become a profound support.

Bowing to your anger

Bowing is universal, but has been honed to an art in the Far East. In Japan, a smartly dressed attendant may bow to you as you enter a department store. Anytime you meet someone there, bowing is part of the greeting. The higher your standing in the community, the deeper people will bow to you. Bowing is a gesture of welcoming, good manners, and most of all, respect. People bow to each other, and to their ancestors, and to their food.

If in doubt, the guide books will tell you, bow.

But how do we bow to our anger, and why? Anger is a strong emotion: it can rise up within us fast and furious, whipping us into a frenzy like a tornado. In the midst of that frenzy, is it possible to simply observe our anger, and to bow to it? Bowing has the effect of pausing, of acknowledging, of respecting, of creating a polite distance. It is the act of saying, 'Hello, anger, I see you are here again and I acknowledge you.' It is the act of realising that the anger is not me.

Actually, this second requirement goes for all of our emotions – grief, anxiety, fear, loneliness, irritation. When we can bow to an emotion, it is no longer able to engulf us. We are not suppressing, but we are also not being crushed. By bowing we are respectful of the power of emotions, but we are also demonstrating that we are not overwhelmed.

Next time strong emotion takes hold, try this: let go of the story that has created the emotion and instead, see if you can bow.

Limiting the sphere of your activity

With perseverance many of us eventually manage to create a schedule we can stick to, and perhaps we even get the hang of bowing when we're feeling furious. But *limiting the sphere* is the key element of practice that, in our modern culture, is the hardest one to master.

Limiting the sphere of activity means:

- letting go of the habit of filling every moment of the diary
- letting go of the urge to take on endless new projects (the 'yes' trap)
- letting go of multi-tasking
- letting go of the habit of justifying our existence through being busy
- letting go of the tendency to get and create more and more
- letting go of the tendency to hurry
- enjoying unscripted moments of the day

This is, frankly, so alien to most of us that at first the best we can hope to manage is perhaps a few moments in the day when we are not rushing somewhere or imagining that we need to be doing anything. A good time to experiment with this is after a mindfulness practice period: if you practise the body scan or seated meditation, try having a bit of time afterwards where you do not have to do anything. This is a 'To Do Free' time zone. It may feel bizarre at first, *but in order to be mindful, it is essential, in the first instance, to slow down.* Limiting the sphere of your activity has two sides: the first is to give up the delusion that multi-tasking is possible or desirable. Instead, we commit to just doing one activity now, giving this our full attention. The result of 'one thing at a time' is that we execute our necessary tasks better, and enjoy them more. The second more long-term aspect of limiting the sphere is that we take on the perspective of a Japanese flower arranger, removing from the bouquet of our life anything that is not essential or nourishing the whole. The result of limiting the sphere is a greater sense of spaciousness, a steadier mind, and a deeper appreciation of each moment of our life.

One time a student asked her teacher how to create a regular practice. 'It's great when I am on a retreat – I get all enthusiastic and really feel this is what I want to be doing, but when I get home, in the midst of work and life, it just tails off. How do I keep going?'

The teacher listened. He paused. He did not give any helpful hints about timetables or transience. Instead he just asked, 'What are you doing right *now*?'

14.
Effort and ease

Today, the earth feels softer. The hard crunch of the icy soil is gone. Instead, shoes impressing, creating tracks in the thin grass. And here, by the path, a miracle. One small white snowdrop, that seems to have come from nowhere. Its petals are closed, folded around each other, not quite ready to open. But it is here, pure white poking up through the mud. And with this one small tentative blossom, the earth offers its promise of renewal.

To practise mindfulness requires some effort. It might be the effort involved in turning up at the class after a long day of work. It might be the effort of finding time and space to practise at home. It might simply be the effort of sitting upright for meditation, even though this does not always feel entirely comfortable. However, understanding what kind of effort we need is a subtle business. If we make too much effort, we risk becoming rigid and stuck. If we don't use enough effort, we will never actually practise. Particularly when we meet resistance, understanding what sort of effort and energy we need is essential. For example, if you are driving or cycling up a steep hill, you need to be in a low gear. This chapter is an invitation to become curious about effort, so that it's possible to use it skilfully, depending on the circumstances that are encountered.

Essentially, there are two broad areas of effort:

1. the effort we need to get us practising
2. the effort we need to use once we are practising, so that we are able to meditate with greater ease

Skilful effort in getting down to practice

For many, it feels great to make a new beginning. We've found something – in this case, mindfulness – and we know from all of the research we've read and what our friends have told us that it's going to make us feel better. We've signed up for the course, perhaps we've even bought a new yoga mat, and within us is that mixed feeling of optimism, anticipation, excitement.

We come away from the first class full of promise. We go home with the body scan recording and the invitation to practise each day, as best we can. We really feel we have the resolve to do this; after all, what could be easier than lying down for half an hour each day and letting go of all the other stuff we have to do?

Practising at home is different from doing it in the class. If we wait till the end of the day, by the time we lie down for the body scan we may just fall asleep. But doing it in the morning involves getting up earlier than usual, and even the thought of that starts to make us feel stressed. When we get home from work is another possibility, but the phone rings and then we need our supper.

Finally we manage to carve out the time and space to play our recording of the body scan, and even manage to stay awake for most of it. But we've heard this recording a few times now, and the words are always the same: how can anyone be expected to listen to the same thing over and over again? We start to imagine that with another recording, things might get better.

The other issue we have is *where* to practise the body scan. The bed is too soft (inviting sleep) and the floor is too hard (our back starts to hurt). So we turn into Goldilocks in the land of mindfulness, searching for the right time and place to practise, and finding that it's always either too early or too late, too hard or too soft ... where oh where is the time and place that's 'just right'?

And at last, when we seem to have sorted out the practicalities of when and where, sooner or later we are faced with something else that derails us. Maybe it's a deadline at work, or maybe we get ill. Whatever it is, our carefully arranged practice routine goes out the window. We just have to deal with whatever problem is going on in our lives, and hope that we will somehow manage to get back to mindfulness when things settle down.

Here's an outline of what is happening:

Initialising energy

We are newly enrolled on a mindfulness course, feeling enthusiastic and hopeful. The energy that arises to help us comes from the feeling that, as mentioned in Chapter 2, we need to make a change. Something is not quite right – and it's important to recognise that this feeling of dissatisfaction with ourselves and our lives is common to everyone. The advertising industry and hundreds of self-help books rely on this fact: that we feel inadequate in some way, and therefore we need to 'fix' or improve ourselves and our circumstances.

Many wonderful aspects of our lives have arisen out of this desire to improve things ... our ancestors harnessed fire, made clothing, invented the wheel, worked clay into pottery, all to make life a little easier. This is the energy that we tap into when we embark on a new course. In this phase our motivation is clear: we want mindfulness to relieve us of our stress or our pain or whatever it might be. The steps we take to sign up and then turn up at the first class do not really feel effortful (unless we are experiencing anxiety or depression) because our hopeful enthusiasm is fired up. We have successfully tapped into our initialising energy.

Sustaining energy

Often after a week or two of a mindfulness course, the initial excitement begins to wear off. This is actually a vital moment in learning about mindfulness, because this is when we first appreciate that now a *different kind of effort is required*. Words such as discipline, commitment and perseverance start to emerge in the mind, and none of these sounds very exciting. The thrill of the beginning (romance) gives way to daily practice (long-term relationship). The hope of finding an instant cure for our ills turns into the reality of seeing perhaps some signs of relief, but realising we have a long road ahead of us in order to be even moderately free from suffering.

The energy we need to begin to discover within ourselves at this point is a kind of patient, open-minded diligence. As scientists, there is no point leaving the lab when the experiment has just begun. Curiosity is required, and a willingness not to judge or jump to any conclusions. After all, we are still learning how mindfulness practice might impact on our lives. Sustaining energy involves a willingness to practise even when we don't much feel like it, as John's story makes clear:

At the end of a long day, I don't really feel like practising. It's easier just to surf the net or watch a film. But I've been having problems with sleep, and I've noticed that if I do some mindful yoga before going to bed, that actually I sleep much better. So although sometimes I don't really want to, I make myself unroll the yoga mat. I might listen to the yoga CD, or I might just start with something simple, like lying on the floor. Once I start, it's surprisingly easy. I enjoy it, and my mind changes gear. And then I sleep. I guess it's knowing that I will sleep that helps me persevere.

Around week two of the course, people sometimes report that they have started to feel 'bored' by the body scan. Boredom is, as discussed in Chapter 8, a form of aversion. Boredom arises when we don't really want to be doing whatever task is at hand. But it is also a sign that we need to dig deeper, and to increase our efforts. In the body scan, it is not sufficient to hear the recorded words: each time we lie down to practise, we need to be genuinely investigating the physical experience of being in our bodies. *The body scan is not an intellectual exercise – it is an experiential practice.* Each time we practise, places in the body will feel different, because our bodies are always changing. There will be an ache or a tingling sensation one day that was not there the day before. Each body scan is a unique opportunity to get more deeply in touch with our physical selves. In this practice, we can let go of any of the normal concerns with how our bodies look: instead, we are discovering the actual felt sense of what it is to be alive in this moment. This means that we start to notice and feel things that we didn't notice before. As one student said:

In the beginning, when the instructions asked us to breathe down the legs, I didn't know what I was supposed to be doing. And then one day I got it. Suddenly, I could send the breath down the legs, and I could feel it actually happening. It was amazing.

Without sustaining energy, discoveries like this one will never happen.

Getting knocked off course

Even when we manage to learn how to approach mindfulness in a deeper way, obstacles will arise. This is an inevitable part of meditation practice. Sooner or later, something will get in the way. If you have children, the school holidays come along and mean that your quiet time is no longer quiet. If you're a teacher, an impending visit from the school inspectors can completely take over every waking (and sleeping) moment. Deadlines, travel, family, migraines – each of us can write a list of the things that knock us off course. And the point about these obstacles is that there is no choice: we just have to manage as best we can. At these moments, there genuinely seems to be neither time nor any mental space in which to practise.

Whenever one of these obstacles appears, it's reassuring to remember three simple facts:

- everyone gets knocked off course now and then
- it's easier to get back on the path if you don't get involved in self-judgment
- even in a crisis, it's possible (and useful) to be mindful

How is it possible to be mindful in the midst of turmoil? Just by noticing. So while there may be no time to meditate for thirty minutes, there is always time to notice how things are. Where is the tension in the body as I wait to start this driving test? Where is the breath? What are the thoughts in the mind, and what exactly is this emotion? How does the air feel on the skin? Making this enquiry can take less time than reading this paragraph, but it offers us the one thing that seems to be lacking when we're overwhelmed: it offers us choice. We can choose to turn towards our experience. And in that act of greeting life just as it is, we gain at least a small measure of control, and reclaim the possibility of being curious. Curiosity is a miraculous antidote to panic.

Renewing energy

This means starting formal practice all over again. Here we reach a critical moment; partly because of doubts that may have crept in, and partly because our energies are quite possibly at a low ebb. At this moment, it's necessary to begin gently, and with clear intention. Experiment with these seven steps when renewal energy is needed:

1. As always, begin with recognition. *I haven't been managing to practise lately.*

2. Let go of any tendency to judge. *Well, I was ill. These things happen to everyone.*

3. Remind yourself of what drew you to the practice. *I took up meditation because everything was getting on top of me, and actually, I was starting to feel like I had more choices, more control. I was a happier person!*

4. Begin gently, with a practice you connect with easily. *I know I always enjoyed the body scan. I'll start there.*

5. Start with a short practice. *I'll just do the ten-minute body scan, and then I'll see how I feel.*

6. Afterwards, don't do anything for a while, and allow yourself some non-scripted spaciousness, perhaps a warm drink or sitting in the fresh air. *Ah, the birds are singing ...*

7. Now choose when, where, and which practice you
   will do tomorrow, and include spacious time after.
   Hey, I might be on track again ...

Successfully negotiating your way through this renewal
process will put you back on track, where you can reconnect
with sustaining energy. At this point, the more regularly you
practise, the easier it becomes, until sitting down to meditate
feels as natural and nourishing as eating or sleeping. This
doesn't mean that things will never again knock you off
course, but it does mean that you will have the confidence
to re-engage with mindfulness after (and even during) the
storm.

Here is a story that demonstrates the importance of knowing
how to start again:

Aaron Siskind was an abstract impressionist photographer –
in simple language, this means that he took pictures of walls.
Mostly these were walls with interesting cracks or bits of
paper peeling off them, and through the photograph, he
allowed people to look and genuinely see the beauty and
meaning in something that they would otherwise have
ignored. Back in the 1970s, he came to host an exhibition
of his work in Oxford.

During one of his talks, someone asked him this question:
'What do you do when you're stuck, when you have a
creative block?'

He answered, 'I go back to a place that worked for me
before – perhaps a particular building or a piece of wall, and
I start there again, photographing, looking, finding inspiration.
Once I get over that initial block and get going again, then
everything starts to flow.'[1]

Skilful effort during practice

Getting down to practice is only half of the story. The other half, in some ways the more mysterious part, is discovering what kind of effort is needed once we are actually in the middle of practising.

Meditation is a sort of balancing act. When we sit down to practise, we need to be upright, and without tension. This external form mirrors what we are aiming for within us – our attention needs to be switched on, but without any sense of constriction. Meditation that is too concentrated will inevitably create physical tension and pain. Meditation that is too slack will result in daydreams, fantasies, boredom or sleep. So practice is about finding a middle way, where we are completely awake and at ease.

Here are two time-honoured analogies that describe this process of finding balance.

Guitar strings

Think of the strings on a guitar or a violin or a ukulele. If the string is too loose, it wobbles all over the fretboard and can't create a proper sound. If it's too taut, it will snap. The string needs to be tight enough to produce a pleasing tone, but not so tight that it's under too much stress. This is precisely the way in which we need to tune ourselves when we practise mindfulness. We need to make a certain effort, in terms of sitting up straight and keeping our attention focused on whatever is happening right now. But we also need to allow a sense of being at ease, both physically and mentally, so that we can sustain the practice. This sense of ease allows us to acknowledge that the attention will wander, combined with the confidence that we can bring it back. In the same way that it's necessary to tune the guitar string, we are continually retuning our minds, training them to return to being in the present moment, here now, over and over and over again.

The Muddy Pond

This time, think of a pond. Perhaps it's just rained, or someone was stirring it up with a stick – in any case, the water is murky. This murky water is like our mind when all of the thoughts are churning around. So the question is, how to create a pond with lovely clear water? Can we make it happen? The answer is: we cannot. We cannot make the water settle. But if we give it time, the mud settles to the bottom of its own accord. Meditation is like this.

We sit still, without interfering, and allow the muddy thoughts to settle. We maintain a watchful attention, so that we don't churn up too many new ideas and plans (there will be a few) and we patiently wait. If we can be patient enough, the mud begins to settle, and the water becomes clear by itself. It wasn't our effort that made the mud settle: we were merely a witness in a natural process. This is meditation. We sit, with attention and curiosity, to see who we are once the mud has settled. No force is needed. We just need to be still and balanced, steady and easeful, and awake. *In fact, even to have the desire that the water should become clear can be an impediment.* And so here is another secret of practice: the best way is just to sit and observe the muddy pond. Bubbles may rise to the surface. Something that we couldn't see at first may come into view. We are not in control, and eventually we even learn to let go of wanting any particular outcome. Here we are, and here is the muddy pond. It doesn't need to be clear: it doesn't need to be anything but just how it is. So we sit and watch, curious and happy to pay attention.

With no idea at all of what we will discover.

15.
The toolkit

Rain, like the sound of polite applause, on the roof of the hut. Mud and puddles and squelch. Most of the birds shelter to keep their feathers dry, but the woodpecker is here, hammering his beak into the peanut feeder, his red underbelly the only bright patch to be seen.

On mindfulness courses, 'toolkit' is a common word. We are given various practices to add to our toolkit. They are all great pieces of kit, but only if we know how to use them. Understanding the intention behind each of the mindfulness practices will help us decide which practice we wish to choose. It may also help us understand and negotiate any resistance that arises in respect of a particular practice. In this chapter, we'll look at each of the mindfulness practices that commonly appear on an eight-week course. You may wish to focus just on the parts of this chapter that relate to the particular practice(s) you are working with at the moment, or on the one(s) that you find challenging.

The full-length practices

The body scan
The body scan is the first formal practice on most mindfulness courses. It involves lying down (or finding another position,

if lying down is not comfortable) and turning the attention to various parts of the body, one at a time. Usually the scan begins with the toes, and moves up from there, through the legs, the torso, the arms and the head, exploring sensations and discovering the body on an experiential level. This practice takes thirty to forty minutes. The purpose of the body scan is essentially four-fold:

- to tune into physical sensations, which brings the mind into the present moment
- to train the attention, moving it from one part of the body to another by intentional choice
- to learn what to do whenever the mind wanders off course (bring it back, non-judgmentally)
- to begin the process of being with any physical discomfort by exploring it without secondary tension or avoidance

Notice that none of these four rationales includes the word 'relax'. This is one of the most common misconceptions that people on mindfulness courses have: that the body scan is intended as a relaxation. But if relaxation is a goal, and something apart from your present experience, then this practice is not about relaxing. If you listen closely to the recorded practice, you will very likely find that the word 'relax' does not appear. The body scan is intended to help us get in touch with however we are at this moment. Restless, sleepy, in pain – it doesn't matter what we are experiencing: what matters is that we become fully aware of it.

Viewed in this way, it becomes clear why mindfulness courses usually begin with the body scan, and why we are asked to persevere with it: the body scan offers us all of the essential building blocks that we need in developing mindful attention. The fact that it often helps us to move into a state of mental and physical ease is just a bit of icing on the cake!

When to use the body scan

If you are just starting out on the mindfulness path, the body scan is helpful in giving you a foundation for practice that will serve you well for all subsequent practices that you learn. It is also a useful practice to start with if you've had a break from practising for a while. It can be a helpful practice in the middle of the night, if you can't sleep – people often report that they listen to the body scan, and are able to sleep well afterwards.

In addition, if the mind is agitated, so that longer silent periods of the seated meditation practices feel too challenging, the body scan has the advantage of offering fairly constant instructions to keep the attention on track. The body scan can also be helpful during illness or while convalescing. Although some places in the body may be unwell, the body scan invites us to discover those other places that are okay, and that we may be ignoring. Marshalling our 'wellness' to nourish those parts of the body in need can be reassuring, as well as healing.

Seated meditation

Seated meditation carries on the work that we started in the body scan. We are still training the attention to stay in the present moment, but now, in addition to paying attention to the breath and body sensations, we may also turn the awareness towards sounds, and towards thoughts as they come and go. At some point, we may also be asked to move into 'spacious awareness', where we simply notice whatever is arising, without focusing on anything in particular.

And there is another key feature to seated meditation – the most important part of all: in this practice, we start to get a feel for what it is like to practise for periods of time in silence, without any verbal instruction to keep us on track.

Why move from the body scan to seated meditation? After all, in both we are using our intention to pay attention to our experience. And yet, seated meditation is different. It *feels* different. Obviously sitting up requires muscular effort that was not required in lying down, but there is more to it than that. In seated meditation there is some quality that is essentially mysterious. Why are we invited to sit up? Why is our posture relevant to the way we perceive and process experience?

When Jon Kabat-Zinn began teaching mindfulness in a hospital in Massachusetts in the 1970s, his meditation instruction was to sit, 'with an erect and dignified posture'.[1] Generally, when we hear this, we sit up a little straighter. But we tend to have so many subtle variations in our habitual posture that it may be useful to have more information. Remember, when you read these guidelines, that they are a direction of travel rather than an absolute you must adhere to, regardless of the discomfort. At all times, the most important voice to listen to, when arranging yourself for seated meditation, is the voice of your own body. (See Figure 3.)

❖ *Sitting in a chair*: If you're not used to sitting on
   the floor, then a chair is probably best. A wedge
   or cushion on the chair will help to tilt the pelvis
   slightly forward, and this in turn helps the spine
   to be naturally upright. If your back will permit it,
   sit away from the back of the chair, so that you are
   self-supporting. The soles of the feet need to be flat
   on the floor – if your legs are short, a yoga block or
   a book under the feet may help. Shins need to be
   straight up and down, with a bit of space between
   the knees, so that there is no holding in the thighs.

❖ *Sitting on a meditation bench*: A meditation bench is
a low wooden bench with a sloping seat, so that
the pelvis tilts forward. If your knees will permit it,
sitting on a bench is surprisingly comfortable, as
it allows the back to be naturally upright, without
much effort. Have a fist-width of space between the
knees. It's useful to have some padding underneath
you on the floor, so that the knees and feet are
cushioned. If the tops of the feet feel over-stretched,
roll up a towel and rest the feet on top of it, so that
they are not flat against the floor.

❖ *Sitting on a meditation cushion*: This is only a good
approach if both your knees and your hips are
flexible. A meditation cushion is usually round, and
firm, and at least 10 centimetres thick. If when you
sit on a cushion you find that your knees do not
rest on the floor, it's better to go back to using a
bench. Meditation requires that we have a firm and
stable base: if your knees are in the air, you will lack
stability, and be prone to pain in the lower back and
thighs. If only one knee is slightly elevated, pop a
rolled-up towel or a yoga block underneath it.

❖ *For all sitting positions, a ten-point guide*:

1. Start with awareness of the sitting bones, and find
   the spot where you feel balanced equally on both
   of them.

2. Now let the tailbone drop, to reduce the curve at
   the waist. This helps the spine to grow up out of
   the pelvis, so that you may become a little taller.

3. Become aware of the spine. Allow it be upright,
   like a plant growing up towards the light. You
   might find it useful to imagine a silk thread

coming from the crown of the head that invites the spine to grow upwards.

4. Soften the shoulders.

5. Lengthen the back of the neck, and pull the chin in slightly, so that it is level. Let the ears be in line with the shoulders.

6. Soften everything below the waist – no holding in the abdomen.

7. Let the hands rest on the thighs. Palms down gives you the sense of being grounded. Palms up creates the quality of being receptive.

8. Eyes open can be useful if you are sleepy or prone to daydreaming. If open, lower the gaze, about a metre ahead on the floor. Let it be a soft gaze, with no intention to focus on anything in particular.

9. Now take in the whole of your being. For meditation, we are aiming for a posture that is awake, upright, and also at ease. If you find holding and tension in the way you are sitting, look for ways of introducing softness and ease.

10. Finally, be aware that while the intention of this posture is the cultivation of stillness, no posture is ever completely static. If you are not used to sitting up, then slumping may well creep in. If you are stressed, tension will arise. Part of being present in meditation is noticing what the body is up to, and making minor adjustments as needed.

Why do we sit like this? One time I asked my meditation teacher this question. He answered, 'Because this is the way my master taught me.'

Figure 3. Three sitting positions

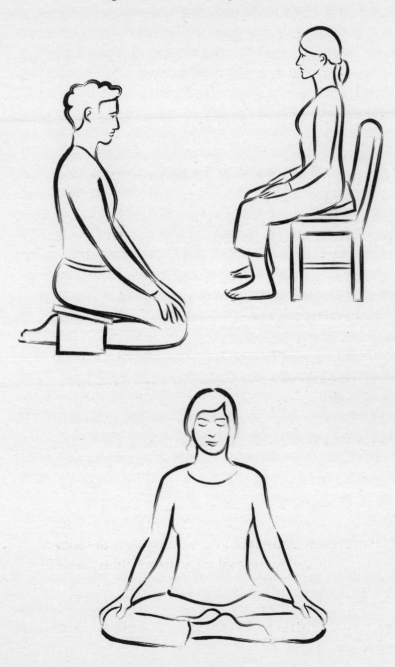

At the time, it did not seem like an entirely satisfactory explanation. In our modern Western culture, if we are going to do something, we want evidence. There is evidence that sitting in an upright and open-hearted manner improves our mood. And once you find your own most stable and comfortable way of sitting, you will find that it is a posture you can maintain for some time without needing to move. We are not leaning forward (into the future) or backwards (into the past). We are here, quiet and stable, in the centre of our unfolding experience.

So why did my meditation teacher say, 'Because this is the way my master taught me'? Because this acknowledges a vital truth: meditation is taught by one person to another. My teacher taught this to me. His teacher taught it to him. His teacher learnt it from his master, and so on, all the way back in the lineage that is at least 2,500 years old. There is something mysteriously potent about sitting upright to meditate. It enables us to hold, witness, and let go of whatever arises within and around us. It embodies a state of balance and equanimity. It helps the mind to become aware and clear. It is a profound gift that each generation of meditators offers to the next generation. Each time you take your seat to practise, you are plugging into this ancient tradition, where each being in that long line of experience is supporting you and wishing you well in your endeavour.

Once you have taken your seat to meditate, pay some attention to your hands. After the face and the voice, our hands are the most expressive part of the body. Therefore, it makes sense to include them in our posture. Here are some possible ways to rest the hands (see Figure 4):

1. Let the palms rest on the thighs in a way that allows the shoulders to be at ease. This position offers a sense of grounding, and of being in touch with ourselves.

2. *Chin mudra:* a second possibility also involves resting the palms on the thighs, this time adding in a 'mudra'. A mudra is a symbol we make with the hands – a kind of statement. In chin mudra, we bring the tip of the thumb and the tip of the first finger together so that they touch lightly, making a circle. This symbolises the individual being in touch with the universal, or our 'historical dimension' being connected to our 'ultimate dimension' (for more on this, see pages 68–70). Again, this position offers a sense of being grounded.

3. *Jnana mudra:* this time we make the same gesture with the thumb and forefinger; the only change is that we rest the back of the hands on the thighs, so that the palms are facing upwards. The difference here is that the hands become more receptive.

4. *The cosmic mudra:* here we place the right hand in front of the lower abdomen with the palm up, and then rest the left hand on top of it. The tips of the thumbs meet, making an oval shape. This gesture is about bringing both right and left to the centre, so that there is no sense of duality. For this position, the hands need to be supported, so depending on how you are sitting, you may need a small cushion in your lap for the hands to rest on.[2]

It does not matter which of these positions you use – choose the one that feels most comfortable and appropriate. The important point is that you are allowing the hands to express the intention and the understanding of meditative practice.

Figure 4. Positions for the hands

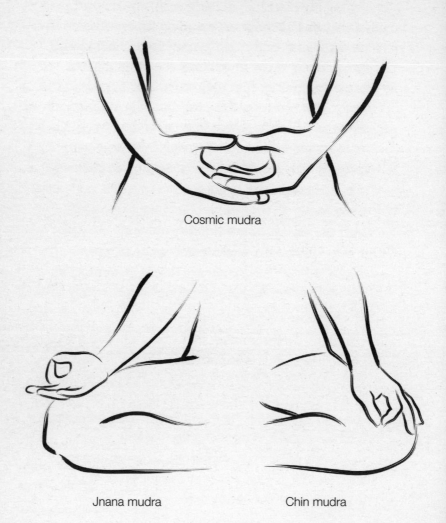

Cosmic mudra

Jnana mudra   Chin mudra

When to practise seated meditation

Once you have got the hang of sitting upright, seated meditation can be practised every day. You will never outgrow it. It is especially useful when times are challenging, and you simply don't know what else to do. Although the seated meditation recording from your mindfulness course will be between thirty and forty-five minutes long, it is not always necessary to sit to the end of the practice. *It is better to sit down for even five minutes, than to feel that you have not sat at all.* With time, the physical aspect of sitting up to meditate gets easier and easier, until it feels like the most natural posture in the world.

Yoga, stretching, tai chi, or ki gung

> *The practice of yoga only requires that we act and at the same time, pay attention to our actions.*

Desikachar[3]

How much movement you learn on your mindfulness course will depend on your teacher. In some classes a full forty-five-minute practice is offered, while on other courses the stretching that you do may be much shorter. Over the years on the courses that I have facilitated, students often report that mindful yoga is one of the most helpful practices they learn.

If we are going to be mindful, we need to be mindful *of* something. In yoga, we use body sensation as our object of awareness. This is often easier for people than sitting quietly and trying to keep the attention focused on the breath.

Yoga is a valuable part of our toolkit for many reasons. Yoga can help:

- relieve pain and stiffness in the body by letting go of unnecessary, unconscious tension
- move out of mental rumination and into awareness of body sensation
- explore the physical limits of the body in a safe way and appreciate that limits change when we stay in a pose
- move out of the physical 'automatic pilot' and become more aware of how we stand, sit and move
- ease depression and improve mood
- let go of competitiveness and the desire to perform
- improve posture and flexibility, which in turn helps us practise seated meditation more easily
- increase awareness of and improve the flow of the breath
- increase mental focus (also good preparation for seated meditation)
- rebalance energy levels: waking us up if we're tired, or helping us settle if we feel wound up
- experience, appreciate and accept our body, just as it is

One of the key features of mindful yoga is that there is no 'trying' to achieve a particular posture. We make a gentle movement, using the breath to guide us, and we pay attention to the sensations that arise. So instead of a goal of how our bodies should look, we are becoming curious about the felt experience of being in this unique body. Mindful yoga unites the breath, the body and the attention. Practised in this way, yoga is a wonderful gateway into awareness. It can also have other unexpected benefits, as this report from Joe illustrates:

> I came on the mindfulness class, hoping to experience some 'peace of mind'. I got this in abundance and a lot more besides. I have suffered from arrhythmia for several years and despite several ECGs and wearing twenty-four-hour monitors, the doctors could not pinpoint anything specifically wrong. My heart beat would quite often race away, and I could feel it thumping hard in my chest, especially at night or when I was in 'quiet mode'. During one of the mindful yoga sessions, I suddenly felt very different. We were lying on our backs with our feet in the air, propped up against the back of a chair. It took me a few seconds to work out what was different – then I realised, my heart was beating absolutely normally. I tried not to get too excited and put it down to a 'one-off'. Over the next few weeks, I kept practising this exercise, and the normal periods of heart beating kept getting longer. Even though I did not dare think I was miraculously cured, I started to have hope. One year on, I enjoy what most people take for granted – a heart which beats normally.

When to practise yoga

If you've been working at a desk all day, then yoga is a great way to offer kindness to the body. Many people find it easier to pay attention in yoga, because the body has something 'to do'. Stretching is also incredibly helpful before seated meditation: it stabilises the breathing, the body and the mind, so that we are more focused when we move into stillness. Gentle yoga can also be helpful at the end of the day, to prepare the body and the mind for sleep.

Kindness meditation

Over two millennia ago, the monks in India who practised meditation often sat alone in the forests. To sit on the earth in the midst of nature is a wonderful way to practise – but there was a problem. The problem was tigers. In the wilds of northern India there were Bengal tigers; and thinking that they might get eaten at any moment made it difficult for the monks to meditate. So they were given *metta bhavana,* or kindness practice. Kindness practice is said to be an antidote for fear, ill will and anger.

Fear includes anxiety, worry, unease, the sense of needing to be in control. Ill will includes any form of aversion (see Chapter 8): boredom, restlessness, rebellion – these are all aspects of ill will. Anger is just that, but also includes more subtle variations, including irritation and indignation. The point with all of these emotional states is that they are within us, poisoning us. They each have a profusion of thoughts attached – *what is going to happen to me if? ... How could she do that to me? ... I just want to get out of here ...* and so on. All of these thoughts pull us away from the present moment, and into a fantasy state of what we will do or what will happen to us.

The Vietnamese Zen Master Thich Nhat Hanh compares anger to our house being on fire.[4] We believe that someone has set our house alight and we're so angry, we want to chase the arsonist and catch him. But all the while, the flames are destroying our house. What we really need to do is look after our house, and put out the fire. So when we are angry, the emotion is within us, damaging us. And the place we need to pay attention to is ourselves, not anybody else: thinking that someone else 'made' me angry and chasing after him is not going to free me from the miserable condition of feeling angry.

This is the purpose of the kindness practice – to free us from the negative emotions that make our lives difficult. Kindness meditation enables us to cultivate a friendlier and more accepting attitude towards ourselves and others: it is not about achieving any particular emotional state. Instead of going over and over all of the terrible things that make us so cross, we move into a different mind-state by using the phrases of friendly awareness:

May I be safe and well.

May I be free from suffering.

May I live with joy and ease.

The practice then moves from ourselves to others, starting with a friend, then an acquaintance, then someone we find difficult, and finally all sentient beings. So we open the heart by sending good wishes to someone we like, and then experiment with someone we don't know, and then someone we dislike. Obviously offering kindness to a person who irritates us is challenging, but this is precisely the point of the practice: to see that even this tricky person has hopes and fears, joys and sorrows, and is struggling with life, just as we all are.

In offering friendly attention to someone we find challenging, there are two important points to bear in mind. First, it's best to start with someone that we find mildly annoying – don't attempt to begin the practice with the most difficult person in your life. Secondly, create a safe space for yourself; for instance, you might, in your mind's eye, position the difficult person on the other side of a lake. This way, you create a buffer zone between you and the person who has caused you pain. Offering kindness is not intended to change the disagreeable person – it is intended to soften the knot of aversion that we harbour within our own hearts. And once we are freed from the animosity within, it is easier to relate creatively with those around us, as Jane's experience demonstrates:

I decided to practise kindness meditation every day as my main meditation. What surprised me most is that, after about three months, I actually ran out of difficult people. It's not that anyone around me had changed; it's just that my attitude changed. I no longer found them so irritating or challenging. And whenever someone said or did something unskilful, I just used it to nourish my practice.

In the final part of the kindness meditation, good wishes are offered to a larger group, sometimes called 'all sentient beings'. What we are doing here is to appreciate that we are all living beings, we are all connected, we all need friendship and to be free from suffering, regardless of where we live on the planet. Practising kindness meditation will not magically end everyone's suffering, but it will give us a sense of being in touch with others through nourishing our compassion. Kindness practice opens us to the deeper reality that we are not alone.

When to practise kindness meditation

When strong emotions are present, kindness meditation can ease the suffering of the heart. When we have been hurt by someone, we need to offer kindness to ourselves, and once we feel stable enough, to offer kindness to the person who offended us. When we are aware of the suffering of others in the world, and feel powerless to help, kindness is a way of connecting with this larger group, and feeling that at least we can offer them our meditative awareness. Here is a story from Saleem, which shows how we can call on the wisdom of kindness at any moment:

I learnt the kindness meditation in class one week – not realising that I would use it so soon afterwards. Within days, I was out driving when I got cut up on the road by a young man driving a white van, shaking his fist at me. Suddenly, unbidden, loving-kindness words came into my head and as he roared off up the road I wished him: 'May you be safe and well, may you live in joy and peace, may you be free from suffering.' The effect was amazing: any upset I felt just completely disappeared. And a powerful realisation came to me – that this angry young man was suffering. Practising kindness not only helped me, but maybe (I hope) it also helped him.

The Shorter Practices

Eating meditation

On an eight-week mindfulness course, this is one of the first practices that you will encounter. Your teacher will offer you a raisin (or something similar) and invite you to look at it, to feel it between your fingers, to listen to it (squishing helps), to smell it, and finally to place it in your mouth, to begin the process of tasting.

Engaging all of our senses with something as humble as a raisin can seem a bit weird at first. The importance of this exercise is to become aware of how most of the time we eat without really noticing or tasting or enjoying. This opportunity, to move out of autopilot and actually appreciate the food we put in our mouths, is a profound practice. Using our senses of sight, smell, touch, hearing and taste when we eat not only transforms the act of eating, it also brings us into the present moment. And it can, as Bella's story illustrates, have surprising consequences:

My dad, who's got into mindfulness, offered to teach me how to eat. I thought this sounded ridiculous – after all, I've been eating for years, haven't I? – but anyway I said yes. So he took an orange, and we each ate our bits mindfully. The colour, the outer skin, the fine skin on each segment, the juiciness, the pulp – he got me to slow down and actually, it was okay. So the next time I went out with friends into town, we went to a fast food place and I thought, I wonder what will happen if I eat this hamburger mindfully. So I tried it. I looked, and smelled (I missed out the listening bit) and tasted, slowing down my chewing so that I could really taste it. You know what? – the more I chewed and actually tasted that hamburger, the worse it started to taste. It was almost like I could taste all of the chemicals in it. To be honest, it was so gross, I couldn't even finish eating it.

Three breaths

Wherever you are, as you hold this book in your hands, please pause ...

Now take three breaths, slowly ... ...

Pay attention to the places in the body that move with the breath.

Allow the whole body to breathe in ... out.

You might even want to close the eyes.

This practice, if you just had a go, probably took less than a minute. And yet it has the magical capacity to call back our dispersed minds and anchor them firmly, miraculously, in the present moment.

Taking three breaths is a practice that even the busiest person can find time for. Try it while sitting in traffic, or while the kettle is heating up, or while you are waiting for a phone call. Taking three breaths is a way of transforming 'waiting time' (when we are not truly present) into an opportunity to enjoy this precious moment. What's fantastic about taking three breaths is that you never have to 'waste' time waiting for something to happen, because you are always here, practising, appreciating, breathing.

When to take three breaths
Anytime. When waiting. Now.

Mindfulness of daily activities

Earlier, in Chapter 3, you may remember Adam's story about paying attention while brushing his teeth. In fact, we can choose to be mindful of any of our activities – taking a shower, chopping vegetables, listening fully when someone speaks to us. Paying attention does not take up any extra time; it simply means that we are genuinely present for the small, everyday moments in our life. And as Jon Kabat-Zinn says, 'These little moments, they're not little – they're *life!*'

The Three-Minute Breathing Space

This practice was developed for Mindfulness-Based Cognitive Therapy (MBCT) courses, as a simple way of opening to our experience, just as it is. It generally has three stages, and in each stage we are investigating an aspect of our experience:

- what's going on in the mind, the emotions and the body
- focusing completely on the breath as it comes into the body ... and goes out of the body (for at least five breaths)
- expanding the awareness to the whole body, with a sense of how we are, where we are, and how we are connecting to our environment

The Breathing Space is called 'three minutes' but actually it can be done in less time, or it can be stretched out to take longer. The purpose of the breathing space is that we get in touch with how we are. We move out of the future, out of the past, and invest our attention into how we are right now. This may sound simple, but we generally spend a good deal of our lives not being fully in touch with how we are. We don't always know what our minds are up to, we don't fully recognise our emotions. We tend to ignore the state of our bodies, unless there is obvious pain. So although the breathing space doesn't take long, it has the capacity of allowing us to pause and recalibrate.

When to use the Three-Minute Breathing Space

When things are getting too hectic, or when you start to feel overwhelmed, the breathing space can be useful as a way of pausing and re-tuning the awareness. Many people use the breathing space at work: people often tell us that they will go to the toilet and just practise the breathing space before returning to their desks. The breathing space can be helpful when you lie down in bed, just to help let go of the day and prepare for sleep. It is also a lovely practice to help you move out of waiting mode and into being. Waiting for an important email? That's a perfect moment for the breathing space.

Walking meditation

Have you ever watched a young child learning to walk? If you have, then perhaps you have some sense of the wonder of that moment when we are first able to balance the entire body upright on two small feet. When we practise walking meditation, it's an opportunity to re-connect with this wonder, and to appreciate the intricacies of each step. Although most of us walk every day without thinking much about it, walking meditation is actually an advanced practice. This is because there are many fine movements going on when we walk, and it takes some training to be able to pay attention to each of them in turn.

How to approach walking meditation

Walking meditation can be a short practice – something that we do for just a few minutes – or it can become an extended meditation. The length of time matters less than the way we bring our awareness to what we are doing.

It's helpful to begin walking meditation by standing and appreciating that when we stand, we are balancing. The act of standing requires fine-tuning at each moment, so that we don't fall over. Once this awareness is established, contemplate taking the first step. Notice which side the body naturally leads with. Notice how the weight has to shift to the stationary leg, so that the leading foot can lift. Notice the movements in the toes, the ankle, the knee, the hip. Breathe in as you lift the foot, take a small step and breathe out as you place it back on the ground. Notice that walking slowly in this way is more difficult, and requires more balance. Take small steps, moving slowly with the breath, for ten or twelve paces. Then you can turn and walk in the same way back to your starting point. Keep the focus on the soles of the feet.

The key point with walking meditation is that we are not walking to get someplace else – we are walking in order to be present in this moment. In order to help reinforce this point, it may be helpful to say silently, as each foot meets the ground, *arriving … arriving.*

Once the fundamentals of walking meditation are established, it's possible to introduce another, more profound aspect of the practice. And it is this: when we walk, we are walking on the earth. We are touching the earth. The earth is our planet, our home. It nourishes us, it provides the air that we breathe, it quenches our thirst. It embraces us with its gravitational field. Without the earth, none of us would be alive. Without the earth, these words could not be written, nor could you be reading them. Although we walk and drive on the earth without much awareness, we rely on it for every single aspect of our existence. Therefore when we practise walking meditation, it can be an opportunity to appreciate our planet. It is easier to do this if you are outdoors, and easier still if you move off the concrete and onto the grass or the sand or the soil. (How many of us can go for days with no direct contact with the earth?) If it's warm, you can even take off your shoes. Stand, and begin to realise your connection with this living, breathing planet. When you take a step, allow that step to show genuine appreciation for the ground that you walk on – as if the sole of your foot were massaging the earth, to show it tenderness and consideration. As you walk, you might even have the sense that the earth is sending you its own vital energy in return. Walking in this way, each step becomes an expression of gratitude, and of love. Thus walking meditation has the potential to transform our view of the world, and our connection to the planet.

When to practise walking meditation

It's possible to shift into walking meditation at any moment when you are walking – so that a journey to the shops becomes a meditation. It's not necessary to walk slowly; instead, just turn the attention to actually being present and alive in the world as you walk.

Walking meditation is also useful at times when the body is uncomfortable in a static position. It is helpful between longer periods of seated meditation. It can also be useful at night: the next time insomnia visits, experiment with getting up and walking slowly, bringing the attention to the breath and to the soles of the feet.

Sometimes on our courses there will be someone in a wheelchair, and what they have taught us over the years is that wheels are not an impediment to walking meditation. Maybe it would be better to call it 'rolling meditation'. In any case, moving up and down, paying attention to the parts of the body that enable the movement, breathing and appreciating the sense of arriving – all of these elements are available to us all.

Labelling thoughts

Although this is not a core practice on most eight-week courses, over the years mindfulness students have reported that thought-labelling is incredibly useful, so it is included here as another bit of kit for your toolbox. It can be especially helpful when the mind seems to be stuck thinking the same thoughts over and over again, or when a particular train of thought is speeding along with such force that it seems unstoppable.

In class, we use a watch to introduce this practice, and we work in stages. (You will need a watch.) These are:

- First, count how many exhalations you have in one minute.
- Next, count how many thoughts you have in one minute. When you notice a thought arising, count it, and return to the breath, until you notice the next thought, and count that one too.
- Now you are ready for the third phase, which is, when a thought arises, notice what kind of thought it is, and label it.

Here are some common kinds of thinking:

- judging
- planning
- analysing
- imagining
- daydreaming
- worrying
- problem-solving
- remembering
- questioning
- visualising
- imaginary conversations
- justifying
- blaming

And so on ... Your own thinking may well come up with other categories to add to the list. The first point about labelling your thoughts is that you can begin to notice that you specialise in certain areas: some of us are planners, others dwell on what happened in the past. The second aspect of labelling thoughts is that the moment we label what is going on in the mind – *judging, judging* or *worrying, worrying* – we create an opportunity to become unstuck. When we label a thought, we step back from its content: '*Oh, another judging thought.*' That's all it is. Magically, the train of thought comes to a halt.

When to use thought-labelling

This practice can be helpful at any moment when you notice the mind churning round and round. Often, in seated meditation, the mind can become extremely active: once we notice this, labelling the kind of thought that is arising will disentangle us, and allow us to return to the present.

Practices for difficult times

Here are two practices that can be helpful when we're faced with challenging, uncomfortable moments. Using mindfulness in the midst of problems is important because we start to realise that:

a) the difficulty is not keeping us from practising – instead, it can become the subject of our practice

b) in turning towards the difficult experience, rather than trying to avoid it, we suddenly have the ability to transform our lives, turning straw into gold

RAIN[5] is a useful tool, a bit like having an adjustable spanner. No matter the size of the difficulty, we can use RAIN to get a grip. There are four elements:

- **R**ecognising
- **A**llowing
- **I**nvestigating
- **N**on-selfing

The first three elements are straightforward. When something is coming up that causes unease, just recognise that this is what's happening: *I'm stressed, because I'm sitting here waiting for the dentist.*

The next step, rather than to push it away, is to allow myself to be as I am, without judging: *Yes, I am feeling really anxious.*

Allowing leads naturally into the investigation of what is happening: *My stomach is tied up in a knot, my hands are sweaty, my breathing feels fast. I'm feeling really apprehensive, and I'd like to just run away.* In the process of investigating, we can begin to look more deeply at why we are struggling: *When I was a child, I had a dentist that really frightened me. The sound of the drill was so scary. I didn't really understand what was going on, and I felt helpless and in pain. But actually, this dentist is a different one, and I have chosen to be here. Pain relief is much better now, and I can say something if I'm not comfortable. I can even practise my breathing while I'm in the dentist's chair, and use mindfulness to let go of the tension – I wonder how well I can do this.*

And the final step, the one it's often hardest to remember, is non-selfing: *Actually, that dentist from my childhood was not trying to hurt me. He was just trying to fix a tooth, and probably it's quite hard to work on a child's small mouth.* This final step is the magical moment, when we free ourselves up from our 'story' and into a larger view where the whole world is not revolving around us – and that is deeply liberating.

Being with difficulty

This is another useful way of working with problems. It's helpful to practise this one a few times, so that when you actually need it, it's easier to remember.

- Bring to mind some difficulty (tip: start with something small)
- Find the place in the body that reacts to this difficulty. Usually there is a place of tension or tightness. If no particular place is evident, then focus on the place where you normally hold your tension in the body
- Now breathe into the tension, and out from the tension. Let the breath be like a massage, or a warm

hand, offering comfort and support to the painful
place in the body

What happens in this practice is that we are 'changing channels'. Instead of focusing on the problem in our mental sphere, we move into the physical, and we begin to look after the physical through breathing. The fascinating truth about human beings is that there is no separation between body and mind – so that when we ease the suffering in the physical, we often find that the mental tension is also reduced.

Discovering what works for you

On a mindfulness course, many practices are offered. We have examined twelve different ways of working with mindfulness, and depending on the course you have done, you may have learnt even more. Clearly, it is not possible to delve deeply into all of these meditations during an eight-week course. Instead, a course offers you a 'buffet' from which you can pick and choose. One reason we are given this buffet is that different practices work for different people. For some, kindness is transformational and the practice they stay with each day. For others, it is the body scan. It doesn't really matter which practice you choose – what matters is finding a practice that feels beneficial and exploring it.

Sometimes, in the process of this exploration, a practice may begin to feel stale. If this happens, just notice, and then perhaps choose a different practice from your toolkit. The extraordinary truth is that, in the eight weeks of your course, you have been given a wealth of information and ways of mindfully meditating – enough to last a lifetime.

16.
About breathing

Today, on filling the feeders, adding a handful of peanuts to the bird table. Almost immediately, a jay appears, first checking out the scene from a nearby branch, before swooping down and then up in an effortless curve to land on the table. He comes and goes, comes and goes, hiding peanuts somewhere deep in the woods.

The breath is fundamental to our existence. Our first act as individuals when we are born is to take a breath. That first breath may well scorch the lungs, but our bodies know instinctively that it has to happen. Taking a breath is also our final act, and when the next inhalation does not happen, we have, at last, 'expired'.

Throughout history, profound connections have been made between our breath and our being. The ancient Greeks considered that the breath, *pneuma*, was part of our soul and our spirit. The Japanese word *ki* (as in *ki gung*) means air, spirit and energy. In Sanskrit the *prana* is the breath, but also the subtle life force in the body. The Chinese character for breath is made up of ideograms meaning 'conscious self' or 'conscious heart'. All of these perspectives suggest that the breath is more than the physical act of taking in oxygen and expelling carbon dioxide. The breath is the link between the corporeal and the intangible; it supports our physical existence, and at the same time connects us to the more subtle dimensions.

Call it the soul, the spirit, the life force, or whatever terminology feels most appropriate. Every time we inhale, the breath is connecting us to ourselves and to the world.

Viewing the breath in this way, it is not surprising that it is, for most meditative traditions, the main focus of attention during practice. What is surprising is that, at least on modern mindfulness courses, very little is said about *how* to breathe. In general we are told to observe the breath, and not much more. This is fine if the breath is ebbing and flowing with ease, but it is not helpful if the breath is disturbed. If the breathing is anxious, and particularly for those who habitually hyperventilate, paying attention to the breath can accentuate the sense that something is wrong – which in turn creates even more anxiety. This can result in a major obstacle to practising: if paying attention to the breath makes you feel even more agitated, then you are likely to avoid doing it, as this story from Angie demonstrates:

I came on the mindfulness course because of anxiety. But from almost the first meditation, the instructions were to focus on the breath. Whenever I pay attention to my breathing, I start to panic – I know it sounds crazy, but I start to think I am not going to be able to breathe. Fortunately, I told one of the teachers about this. And she suggested that I stop focusing on my breath. Instead, I started to focus on sounds. Because this was something outside my body, it made me less anxious. I only really got the hang of meditation when I stopped worrying about the breath.

Because issues like this one can arise around breathing, this chapter offers a gentle exploration of the breath.

In Chapter 3, the autonomic nervous system was explained. To recap, when we are in 'fight or flight' mode the sympathetic nervous system is operating. In contrast, when we are in a state of ease, the para-sympathetic nervous system has taken over. Breathing is regulated by this autonomic nervous system: when we are in fight or flight much of the breathing is done by the muscles of the upper chest. When we are at ease, most of the breathing is done by a muscle called the diaphragm.

The diaphragm is a bowl-shaped muscle that lies horizont- ally in the body, at the base of the lungs, and sitting on top of the stomach and the liver. When we breathe in, the diaphragm contracts, and moves down into the abdomen, which opens up the lungs. When we breathe out, the diaphragm releases back up into the ribcage, and the lungs get smaller, which creates an exhalation. Two stems pull the diaphragm down into the abdomen, and these also attach the diaphragm to the lumbar spine. These stems contract, the diaphragm is pulled down, and the lungs open. *This means that when you breathe in, in a relaxed state, the belly expands, and when you breathe out, the belly deflates.*[1]

Have you ever seen a baby lying on its back, just breathing? Babies (when they are not upset) are accomplished diaphrag- matic breathers – which means that we all instinctively knew how to breathe with our diaphragms, once upon a time.

As we get older, we acquire many habits: about how we stand and what we eat, and also, how we breathe. Especially if the main goal is to look thinner, then the thought of letting the belly expand is unwelcome. So we end up holding our stomachs in, and the diaphragm ceases to be able to operate properly. The breath gets pushed up into the chest, and when we are chest breathers, we start to hyperventilate. When we hyperventilate, the arteries in the brain contract, which can cause headache and poor concentration. The oxygen we take in is not released to the cells that need it, and this results in feeling dizzy and breathless. The arteries in the body contract, which can cause cold hands and feet, and even trembling.

Muscles become tense. We end up with insufficient carbon dioxide, which creates over-excited nervous and emotional reactions. Here are some of the symptoms of hyperventilation, according to the Journal of the American Medical Association:

> Fatigue, exhaustion, palpitations, rapid pulse, dizziness, visual disturbance, tingling and numbness, shortness of breath, yawning, chest pain, lump in the throat, anxiety, insomnia, nightmares, impaired concentration and memory, and a sense of 'losing one's mind'.[2]

How do you know if you are tending towards hyperventilation? The number of breaths you take in a minute is a guide: 12 to 14 breaths per minute for men, and 14 to15 per minute for women, is considered normal. If you are breathing much more than this each minute, than you may well not be using the diaphragm effectively.[3]

But here's the problem: if you think there is a *right* way to breathe, and if you also think that you are not breathing in that way, it may not be that easy to correct it. Our breathing is habitual – we don't generally give it any thought; it just happens. And if it has been happening for many years without engaging the diaphragm, then learning to use the diaphragm again is going to take time. It requires attention, kindness and, most importantly, an attitude of inviting rather than forcing.

If you'd like to explore your breath, here are some exercises:

1. Experimenting with the position of the breath
Sit in a chair, so that you are upright, and at ease. Place the palm of one hand on your chest and the other hand on your belly. Start by breathing into the chest, so that you feel the hand on the chest moving (don't do it for too long). Notice what happens to the length of the breath and how it makes you feel.

Now change your breathing so that you are breathing into the belly – let the belly expand a bit when you breathe in, so that you feel the movement with your hand. Again, notice what happens to the length of the breath, and how breathing abdominally affects your emotional state, and your mind.

2. Discovering the diaphragm

Again, sit in a chair. With the tips of your fingers, feel just under the bottom of the ribcage. Hold your fingers there, and now cough. You will feel part of the body ballooning out against

Figure 5. The diaphragm

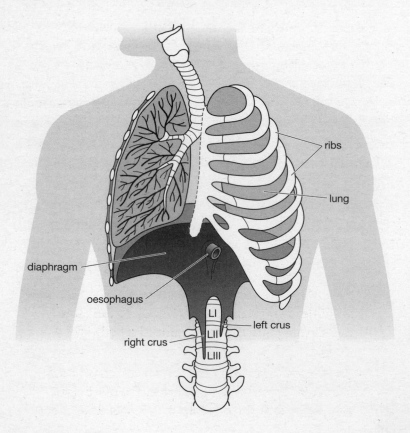

your fingers: this is your diaphragm! You can try it again at the sides of the body, and even at the back. Being in touch with the diaphragm in this way may give you a better sense of how to let it move when you breathe.

3. Observing the breath

There are many aspects to the breath that you can notice. Here are a few:

- Which part of the body moves most when you breathe?
- Where does the breath start in the body?
- Does the breath feel fast or slow?
- Notice the length of the in-breath, the length of the out-breath, and the length of any pause at the end of the out-breath
- Does the breath feel smooth or jagged?
- Does the breath feel shallow or deep?

4. Using awareness of the breath

Once we become aware of the breath, we can use this awareness to help us approach and maintain greater equanimity. Here are two ways to do this:

- Experiment with breathing into the back (especially the lower back). The movement of the breath here is subtle, so it takes some attention to tune into it. Breathing into the back calms the body and the mind.
- Experiment with initiating the movement of the breath in the abdomen. Lengthen the out-breath slightly, so that the exhalation is longer than the

inhalation. This sends a message to the autonomic nervous system to move into a state of greater ease.

Through mindfulness practice, we learn to befriend the breath. Allow it to become an ally, an anchor, a teacher. Receive its constant and subtle messages. Work with it, and it will enliven every single cell of the body.

17.
What goes on in the mind?

Today the sun shines in so low and strong that it is difficult to see. The sedge leaves glisten, the rain puddle glints, the birds sing with renewed intensity. Iris spears have appeared out of the bog, sharp and determined. Sunlight gives the woodland a depth and glow it has lacked for many months. Everything – including this body – feels alive, as if it is smiling.

What happens to the mind when we meditate? The basic answer to this question is that we do not know. One person may be able to notice some of the activity of his own mind, but this does not mean it will be the same for anyone else. Still, it is useful to have a general sense of what might be happening, so that at moments when we think we are 'failing', we can appreciate that we are actually encountering part of the natural process that arises in practice.

Phases of meditation

In the classical texts on meditation, various 'stages' are described, each one leading to a deeper experience of absorption. There might be nine of these, or sixteen, or some other number, depending on the tradition. However, for mindfulness practitioners, most of these states are so 'advanced' that to think we ought to be trying to experience them just puts us back into our goal-orientated habit energy, and will end up making us feel frustrated.

So instead, here are the three states that you will most likely discover as you practise mindfulness.

- The first stage is where we are at the moment. When we begin to practise, what we notice first is how busy the mind is: how it is making lists and plans, how it is chewing over the past, how crazy and jumpy and hyperactive it is, like an incorrigible puppy. Don't feel disheartened when you notice this – because you are beginning to be aware of how the mind normally behaves, and this is the first step on the path.

- The second stage of practice may arise at some point if you persevere; this occurs when the 'doing' mind slows down. In this stage, it may be that our 'puppy mind' of frantic activity has worn itself out and is falling asleep. When this happens, what takes its place is something called the 'Default Network'.[1] As the name suggests, this is a series of other places in the brain that become active when the normal 'doing mind' is quiet. When we are in the default mode, our thoughts are more like daydreams. Ideas, images, fantasies just seem to bubble up unexpectedly. Sometimes it can be a wonderful creative notion, and at other times, it can just be like drifting on a warm sea. The default network is generally a more peaceful part of the brain than the 'doing mode', but it tends to seduce us into a dreamy state. Although the default mode is not generally present-moment awareness, it does indicate that the brain has shifted out of its habitual overdrive. Therefore, it is useful to notice when this state is arising.

- Awareness. In between the thoughts of the doing mode, or the daydreams of the default mode, there are gaps. In the gaps, we drop into the experience of simply being present. In mindfulness we seek to really notice these gaps, and to encourage them. Here is a story to explain this:

A student once asked his teacher how to meditate. The teacher said, 'You know those gaps between one thought and the next? Well, make them bigger.'

We work on appreciating these gaps because, in that pause between one thought and the next, there is stillness. In that gap, the puppy mind is not trying to drag us off course. In that moment, we can drop into being here now. It may be only a brief hiatus before the next thought rushes in ('Hey, I'm not thinking!) but it means that we begin to taste pure awareness, and to know that it is possible.

Sometimes in practice, the movement of the mind takes another route. On this pathway, we are not drifting into daydreams. Rather, because we begin to notice the activity of the mind (as in stage one, above) we move into a more active relationship with thinking; in other words, we begin to think about our thinking. This meta-thinking is still thought, but it is more observational, and less caught by the 'story' of any given thought. Meta-thinking is a useful step because although we are still in thinking mode, we are moving towards the present moment. We are noticing what the mind is doing *now*. This meta-thinking is especially easy for therapists: they tend to be experts at noticing the thought process, and then analysing it.

Of course, there is still another step to take: to let go of the analysis and to move into awareness. Awareness does not need words. It does not involve analysis. It is just this experience.

It is the part of our mind that is larger, broader than the thinking mind. It is our witness. It is a mirror, reflecting without distortion whatever activity is in front of it. And when that activity passes, the mirror does not hang on to what is no longer here. It is always reflecting the now. Just this. Therefore, whatever map or pathway you find yourself on, don't stop halfway. Don't get distracted by the daydreams, or by thinking about your thoughts. The process of the mind when we practise

Figure 6. Two models of the mind during meditation

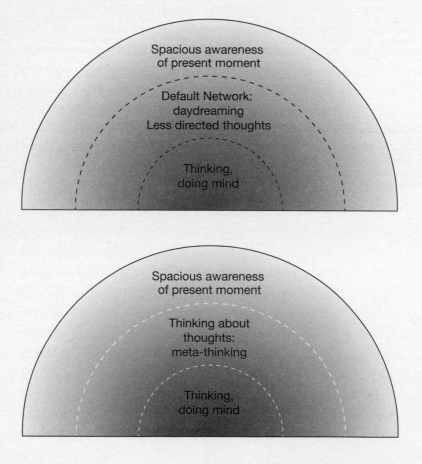

meditation is not linear: it will keep shifting from one phase to another, to another. Whatever stage you find yourself in, keep returning to the breath, and to the sensations that the body offers you. How does the air feel on your skin, just now? Paying attention to this simple, available experience opens us up to the breadth and the stillness and the stability of our human awareness. This is how we can discover the wonder of being alive.

The
Fifth
Secret

Understanding that Support is Vital

18.
Finding the support
we need

Suddenly, in the clearing, two young spotted deer.
They bounce into view, and then, just as fast, they
change direction, leap over the undergrowth, and are
gone. They were here for less than a second, but the
sense of them – fleeting and free – remains.

It is clear that maintaining a mindfulness practice in the midst of our daily lives is a genuine challenge. Traditionally in societies in the East where monks and nuns practise meditation, lay people are not expected to practise at all. It is enough for them to offer donations, attend festivals and follow simple, ethical guidelines. This means that the community of mindfulness practitioners we are part of – living lives that involve work and family and money, while at the same time taking on the practice of meditation – is creating something quite revolutionary: we are making a new template, whereby we incorporate meditation into the midst of day-to-day secular living. This is tremendously exciting; but in order to succeed in this revolution, we need help and support. This chapter investigates some ways to find that help.

Inspiration

Did you ever have a teacher who inspired you – someone who was passionate about her subject, who cared about her students, who helped you to excel? We owe a huge debt to these teachers: they shape our lives. In the field of mindful meditation, there are many wonderful teachers. When we see them, share practice with them, watch them walk or lift a cup of tea to their lips, we know that we are witnessing an embodiment of awareness, and the joy that it brings. To be in the presence of such a teacher is an enormous gift: it becomes possible to understand the true depth of the practice in a way that we cannot glean from books. They inspire us to practise, because we can see so clearly the fruits of the practice in their being.

If you have the good fortune to meet an inspiring meditation teacher, listen and watch and receive. A single meeting may light the fire of your own practice and keep it burning for many years. But remember not to get 'hooked' on the teacher. There is an old Zen saying about a finger pointing to the moon. The teacher you have encountered is a finger pointing to the moon: be sure to keep your eyes on the moon (on the path of mindful practice) and not on the teacher.

Once the fire of inspiration is alight, it is not just a great teacher that we can learn from. The cobwebs in the grass, the sound of the rain, the wind on our faces, a wonderful book – the world offers us inspiration in so many forms, if only we take a little time to notice.

One time, my teacher, myself and a fellow student travelled by train to another part of Japan. On arrival at a station by the sea, the teacher led us up hundreds of stone steps to an ancient temple. Someone was living there, a friend of his, who made us a meal. Later on in the evening another monk suddenly appeared in the room. Did my teacher know he was going to be there? – I am not quite sure. The monk was called Murakami-san. I cannot tell you how old he was, or even a single word that he said. But there was a glow about him, an ease, a clarity, so profound and powerful that it completely stunned me.

We stayed the night, and when we were standing on the train platform the next morning, I asked my teacher, 'What is it about Murakami-san? He seemed to illuminate the whole room. How in the world does anyone become like that?'

Practising with others

Finding a group of people to practise with is, for many, the single most useful key to supporting our ongoing mindfulness. In Buddhist circles this is call 'Sangha' – and it is the community we create in order to sustain each other in our meditation.

If you've already attended a mindfulness course, you've probably discovered that it's easier to practise in class than at home. You can leave the distractions of work and home behind, you know you're in a safe place, you know that this particular time is for meditation. The energy of the group is deeply supportive. Although you may not know these people all that well, you have heard snippets – you know that they are suffering in various ways, just like you. The fact that all of you come together in a circle and dip into the inner silence of meditation is surprisingly special. You are sharing something that feels magical, even sacred. This is the power that arises when we share the practice with others. This story from Dan, a former sceptic, helps to explain the importance of practising with others:

I had always mocked the notion that meditating in a group created any kind of special 'energy'. But I went along anyway, because I was in a lot of pain. I remember they started off by doing some stretches, and I just had to sit and watch.

At the end of the evening, I heard a voice say: 'I just want to thank you all for being here with me, meditating even though I can't do the exercises. I am finding it incredibly helpful and good.' I looked round to see who was speaking, and found it was me!

Finding a group to practise with will depend on where you are. In some urban places, you will be spoiled for choice, with one or another group meeting most evenings. In other settings, you may be fortunate if you can find one person who is willing to sit with you once a week. One person is enough. You can listen to one of your practices from class, and afterwards perhaps share a cup of tea. If you've found an inspiring passage in a book, this is the friend you can share it with. If you are struggling with your meditation, this is the person who will understand.

Over years of practising, there will be lean times – times when not much seems to be happening, times when you wonder about carrying on, or times when your practice grinds to a halt. At these times, having another person that you can practise with will make all the difference. If you are sitting with other people, then when you practice, you can appreciate that you are supporting them. You go along to the group because you care about them, and because your collective energy has the power to heal each one of you. This is another reason that being part of a group is important – because meditation is never something that we do just for ourselves. When we meditate, we are connecting to, and practising with, the whole of humanity. Our meditation group is the concrete manifest-ation of this fact.

If you live in isolated circumstances, it's still possible to create the sense that you are part of a community when you practise. You might agree to meditate at the same time as another friend, even though both of you are not in the same town. Or you might have some photographs set out in front of you, helping you to connect with other people you care about, or are inspired by. The essential element in all of this is to develop the awareness that you are not alone – and that practising mindfulness is connecting you to the whole world.

Research

Each time we sit down to practise meditation, it is an experiment. We create certain external conditions, and then, like scientists, we observe what happens. This is one of the reasons that meditation is fascinating – because we never know what is going to arise. So we each have our own individual research going on within the laboratory of our being.

These days there is also a substantial amount of high-quality scientific research into mindfulness. It has shown that mindfulness eases chronic pain,[1] reduces high blood pressure[2] and psoriasis,[3] and slows the ageing process of the neo-cortex of the brain.[4] Mindfulness has also been found to ease stress, reduce the likelihood of depressive relapses,[5] and lessen anxiety[6] and the tendency towards anger.[7] Mindfulness practice even improves our immune systems.[8] For many people, these findings are reassuring: indeed they may be the reason that they decide to attend a mindfulness course. If enthusiasm is flagging, having a look at the research may help you to redouble your efforts to practise. The important point about many of the studies, especially those that look at the workings of the brain, is that we don't really know what is going on when we practise. We can't actually *feel* that the left pre-frontal cortex is becoming more active or that the amygdala is shrinking,[9] but we may notice after some time that we feel less disturbed by the things that used to upset us. Research tells us that meditation has a profound effect on the shape and function of our brains: and this is utterly amazing. Given this evidence, how could we *not* want to practise? As the poet Rumi, a thirteenth-century Sufi mystic, writes:

> A little while alone in your room
> Will prove more valuable than anything else
> That could ever be given you.[10]

Creating a place

It's true that meditation is possible anywhere – on a bus or a plane, lying in the bath, eating a meal. Still, in order to support your formal practice, it's helpful to have a specific place that you set aside. When you go to this place, it is here, already waiting for you, with everything that you need (chair or bench or cushion) in order to practise. It does not need to be a whole room – a corner of the bedroom will do. The important thing is that it is always available for you. Each time you sit down to meditate in this place, it gets a little easier. The environment supports you – almost as if the place holds the energy of your practice.

Creating a place is also about creating a commitment to your ongoing mindfulness practice. It is an act of intention, and one that you can physically see each day. Think about what you would like to have in this place – perhaps a photo or a flower or a stone. Let it be a place that is simple, pleasant, inviting.

Bite-size practice

Often the biggest obstacle to practising is within us – our attitude towards what is 'enough': *If I can't do a full forty minutes, then there is no point.*

Appreciating that even a short practice is worthwhile can be an enormous support. For example, when we give our full attention to the Three-Minute Breathing Space, we demonstrate to our inner critic that we *can* practise. As Sam, who's been practising for many years, said:

I do try to sit for a full practice, but on the busiest days, it's really not possible. On those days, I sit down and follow the breath, even if it's only five minutes. The difference between five minutes of practice and no practice at all is huge.

Self-compassion

Mindfulness is essentially a compassionate act. Any time we practise, we are offering kindness to ourselves, and to the world. Approaching mindfulness in this way (rather than as something I 'ought' to do) transforms practice from a burden into a pleasure. The key is the realisation that we must look after ourselves if we are to be effective in helping others. In this way, our practice becomes as essential as eating or washing or getting enough sleep.

Going on retreat

One of the great things about an eight-week mindfulness course is that, by the end of it, many students have the understanding and the confidence to go on retreat. A retreat involves joining a group of people in a practice centre, and following a schedule of meditation each day for a few days or a week. Usually there is a teacher who guides the retreat, who will give talks and answer questions. Retreats can be challenging in terms of the demands they make on the mind and the body, but they are also tremendously refreshing. Quite simply, the view you have of the world and your life can be transformed by a week-long retreat.

What is your deepest wish?

Earlier, this question arose as a way of negotiating obstacles to practice. Here it is again, as one of our strongest supports. This question is like the north star, always present to help us navigate our path. Notice that each time you listen deeply to the question, the answer may change. There may be times when there does not seem to be a clear answer – and that is fine too. There is no 'right' or 'wrong' answer. We just need to allow the question to be within us, and to recognise its importance in our lives. Tuning into our deepest wish is one of the best supports we have on the path of mindfulness practice.

The
Sixth
Secret

Seeing the Path
All Around

19.
Signposts

This one small drop, perched on the curve of sedge,
reflects the whole world.

Once a mindfulness course is over, and we have the tools to carry on practising, we need to be more self-reliant. Inevitably at this point, questions arise around the practice: *Is it going okay? Am I still on the right path? How do I know if I start to miss the point?* Traditionally, people practising meditation would have had a teacher to keep them from straying into self-delusion, but these days many mindfulness students do not have access to such a guide. Therefore, this chapter is intended to provide some signposts, so that you can gauge for yourself if you are still on track. Be aware that each of the nine categories here represents a spectrum of possibility; therefore, as best you can, avoid the common tendency to think in terms of black and white. Most of the time we are somewhere in the middle, and the important point to recognise is the *direction* we face as we stand on any of these spectrums of possibility.

1. Wholeness and wholeheartedness *(moving away from dispersion and ambivalence)*
Wholeness arises whenever we pay attention. Just by noticing what is happening *now*, we bring our whole being – body, mind, emotions, energy – into the present. In contrast, when we are thinking about six different things that we know we have to do, our energy is dispersed and distracted, and we're more likely

to feel stressed. Think of the most recent meal you ate: how was the taste and feel of the food in your mouth? Think of a short journey that you took earlier. Did you notice anything about the journey, or how the air felt on your face ... or was your mind completely immersed in what you were going to do upon arrival? These simple, everyday activities call to us, asking us to pay attention to them. And paying attention is not difficult; it is only *remembering* to pay attention that is a challenge. However, when we do make the effort to remember to be mindful, when we do align our minds with our actual experience, we become whole.

Cultivating wholeness in our approach to our lives does not mean that we will get less done; in fact, it will probably make us more productive, and certainly provide a greater sense of satisfaction. The key here is to just do one thing, and to do it with full attention, even if it is a simple task like washing the dishes.

If wholeness has to do with the way we pay attention, then wholeheartedness has to do with our *intention*. Wholeheartedness arises as we create the intention to be fully committed to whatever we might be doing. When we are wholehearted, there is nothing else on our minds; there is no voice inside saying, 'But really you ought to stop and do something else.'

Wholeheartedness is essential to mindfulness practice. There is no point practising the body scan if the entire time you are wishing you were out with your friends. Wholeheartedness requires diligence, and a willingness to let go of other parts of our lives, so that we can just focus on the activity in front of us. When we are wholehearted, it is because we really care about what we are doing.

The other end of the spectrum from wholeheartedness is ambivalence. The ambivalent mind says, 'Well, I guess I will do this practice, but I'm not sure how much I want to engage.' Possibly many of us feel a bit that way when we sit down to practise meditation, and often times, practising itself begins to lead us towards a more wholehearted attitude.

If you find yourself on the see-saw between feeling fully committed and ambivalence, the most important thing you can do is to notice. Notice that the attitude is ambivalent. Notice any thoughts around that ambivalence. Appreciate that probably this feeling of not being sure is something that is an aspect of other parts of your life. Be mindful in enquiring into ambivalence in your life. In this way, the obstacle (ambivalence) becomes the focus of your practice. Be wholehearted in finding out about your ambivalence!

2. Curiosity *(moving away from fear)*
Here is a story about balancing curiosity and fear:

At the beginning of the twentieth century, Native Americans were still living in the wilds of northern California. Their greatest fear was the train that ran through their territory: they believed that it was an angry belching monster which swallowed people whole. One day, the last remaining member of a particular tribe walked into a small town. He was called Ishy. This created quite a stir, as Ishy was naked – so the sheriff locked him up. An anthropologist from San Francisco heard about this, and decided to come and rescue Ishy, as he was the last of a vanishing way of life. The anthropologist took Ishy (now clothed) to the station to wait for the train back to the city. Ishy watched the train approach, and boarded it without any visible trepidation.

Later, once the anthropologist had interviewed Ishy and realised his people's fear of trains, he said to him, 'But how did you manage to board that train with me, without being terrified?'

Ishy replied, 'In my life, I have learnt to be more curious than afraid.'[1]

More and more people who attend our mindfulness course are suffering from fear, anxiety and panic attacks. When we're feeling anxious, anything can seem threatening. A sudden sound, a stranger, a new situation, a deadline, a crowd, a lift, a change in our environment – once the system is fired up to react to danger, virtually everything that we encounter appears to have the potential to harm. This reaction is a form of 'autopilot' of our nervous system, and it gives us the basic message that the world is not safe and we are vulnerable.

Through the practice of mindful meditation, this 'fight or flight' reaction begins to quieten. It becomes, with time, possible to notice a situation and not to react with a heightened state of alert. The reality is that most of the things that make us anxious are not life-threatening: a deadline, or giving a talk in front of strangers – these situations do not put our lives at risk. Once we bring our awareness to this fact, our nervous system learns that it does not have to react to every small provocation. If you have begun to notice this effect – perhaps even that you don't jump when the phone rings – then it is a good indicator that you are on the right track with your practice.

As Maria reported:

One day, I was doing seated meditation, when I heard an almighty crash in the kitchen. It took a split second to realise what it was: the kitchen ceiling, which was damp from a leak in the bathroom upstairs, had finally collapsed. The strange thing was, once I knew what it was, my immediate impulse was to carry on until the end of the meditation practice. The thought was, 'I'll just finish this practice, and then I'll clear up the mess.' So I did. In fact, by the end of the practice, there were moments when I wasn't even thinking about the ceiling any more.

3. Meeting and allowing (*moving away from avoiding*)

Meeting the pleasant moments in our lives is not usually a problem: if a good friend rings and invites us to meet up, we are eager to go. But if a tooth is in pain, how long do we delay in ringing the dentist? For each one of us, the bits of life we avoid will vary – it might be cleaning the house, or paying a bill, or answering certain emails. It might be making a difficult phone call. Whatever the particulars, this general aspect of being human remains the same: there are things in our life that we would rather not do.

Avoidance is not only about chores; it arises also when we are in physical or emotional pain. Part of us would rather not experience that pain. And so we take painkillers, or we distract our attention in some way – and while both of these strategies have their place, neither one of them involves turning towards our suffering.

Why should we want to turn towards the pain? Because this is the only way to gain knowledge, and to allow for trans-formation. If, for example, I can turn towards a headache, and allow myself to pay attention to it, I will begin to notice the details of the pain. What is the sensation actually like? Where is it most intense, and does it travel down my neck, and what happens to the sensation if I change position? This turning towards may not stop me from taking a painkiller, but it does give me a different way of relating to the discomfort while it is here. It also means that, although I cannot control the pain, I can work with my attitude towards it. Instead of just reacting with 'I don't want this headache', I can, through my willingness to be intimate with the sensations, find a place of peace in the midst of the discomfort. And through this turning towards, I begin to let go of the tension that arises in the body when my reaction is, 'I don't want'. This creates confidence and the sense that I am not being victimised by the discomfort. In essence, although I may still be in pain, I have let go of the suffering around the pain. The same goes for emotional and mental pain. By moving in closer to the experience, it is possible to lessen the intensity of our suffering. This is not an easy practice, but it is profoundly worthwhile.

Allowing follows on from the willingness to meet whatever is arising. Allowing says, 'This is how it is right now: I'm feeling stressed and wound up and exhausted.' It might appear that allowing will not solve our problems, but actually it is a vital key. In allowing things to be as they are, we let go of a huge struggle. The struggle lies in the conflict between how things are, and how we want them to be. This struggle is one of the most universal in human nature: we all feel dissatisfied, we all want our lives to be better in some way. Realising that this dissatisfied gloss is something we are likely to apply to any situation – no matter how good things are – is a profound real-isation. It allows us to begin to experiment with stopping, and just allowing things to be.

Allowing is not resignation. It is not about giving up. In fact, seeing the world just as it is, with its beauty and its blemishes, is an essential first step if we truly want to work towards making the world a safer and more peaceful place.

4. Experiencing *(moving away from our personal 'story')*
Mindfulness is an experience. It is the experience of this moment. This moment is always here, within us and around

us, so mindfulness is simply about noticing that we are here, alive and breathing and experiencing, in this moment. There is no other moment that we can directly experience. Here it is, right now. Don't miss it!

But we do. We are missing it most of the time. We are missing it because of the narrative that we have of who we are and what we are trying to get. The narrative, as mentioned in Chapter 12, is *The Story of Me*. In this story, 'I' am the main character: 'I' am the centre of the universe. In the story, 'I' have a beginning, and a linear direction of travel through life. 'I' have likes and dislikes. 'I' have desires and fears. 'I' have things I believe I must have in order to be happy. 'I' have a history: perhaps traumas and incidents that seem to shape who I am. 'I' have a notion of what I can do, and what I can't. This is who 'I' am. And who 'I' am is a fixed entity, with a solid centre, separate and different from everyone else.

The historical sense of self is both persuasive and comforting. Our minds travel up and down the timeline of our life: wandering back into memories of when we were young … wandering forward into the hopes and anxieties that we have about the future. On the historical plane, our minds spend almost no time in the present moment. It is almost as if this moment, with whatever is unfolding in it, will not be interesting enough to feature in *The Story of Me* until it becomes the past.

Through the practice of mindfulness, we are able step out of our personal histories, and into the experiential realm. In the experiential realm, the historical perspective dissolves. We are just here, noticing, open, curious. We are not bound by any notion of who we are, or what we believe we are capable of. Anything could happen. This experiential awareness is always unfolding, just now. It unfolds without language, without the need for an ongoing narrative. It does not require judgment

145

or analysis: instead, it thrives on curiosity. The experience is always changing. We never know what will happen next.

But there is a problem: we do not, in general, feel comfortable with uncertainty. One of the reasons that we prefer to stick to 'the story of me' is that it seems to have solidity. Curiously, it is often at a moment when this solidity crumbles that people decide to begin mindfulness practice. Many people sign up for a mindfulness course after they have been made redundant, or had a marriage break-up, or lost someone close to them, or been diagnosed with serious illness. All of these events have the same outcome: we come face to face with uncertainty. We are no longer in control. We don't know how things are going to be, and we don't know how we are going to cope.

Mindfulness is incredibly useful in uncertain times. The most essential understanding that arises through the observation of each moment is that *everything changes*. Mindfulness won't stop the changes happening, but through learning to inhabit the experiential realm, it does offer us the perfect strategy to help us cope.

5. Resilience *(moving away from feeling overwhelmed)*
As our practice continues, we may well discover that we have grown more resilient. Instead of imagining that each new or challenging situation is going to be a catastrophe, something within us is willing to approach the problem with greater mental flexibility. This does not mean that we embrace each pain or sorrow with open arms, but it does mean that we can meet our life, however it is. Our well-laid plans may be flying out of the window, but we are able, through being present, to have a sense of inner equilibrium. We work out a way of managing and we get through. Afterwards, once the adrenaline wears off, we begin to let go and move on. In other words, we are not stuck. This cognitive adaptability is what makes us

more resilient. You probably won't have time to notice yourself being more resilient in the midst of a crisis, but you may notice it afterwards, when you seem to 'bounce back' with greater ease. This quality of resilience is another clear signpost on the path of mindfulness.

6. Gratitude (moving away from complaining)

Have you ever found yourself in conversation with someone, and noticed that everything your friend says is a complaint? We all have this tendency to a certain extent, but for some people, it is the filter through which they perceive every situation. The weather, the government, the media, the youth of today, the traffic, the potholes, waiting times, flood defences, targets, etc. Complaining is part of our habit energy. Complaining is a form of judgment. It is a way of not taking responsibility, of blaming others. But perhaps most significantly, it is a way of not looking deeply, and of choosing not to understand the difficulties which have helped to create any given situation. It is easier, and more satisfying, just to get up on our soapbox, to take a black and white view of things, and complain.

Here is a warning: mindfulness, if you persevere with it, will undermine your tendency to complain. And in between the gaps, where previously a moan might have arisen, something else will emerge. This something else is gratitude. Gratitude is a bit like a dandelion: you might start off with one, but before you know it, you find a multitude of bright yellow flowers, each one of them another aspect of your life that you feel grateful for. Simple things, like your hands, that allow you to get dressed and use your phone. Beautiful things, like the blossoms on a tree. Huge things, like the earth, that supports your life. Momentary things, like the smile of a child. Things that previously you complained about, like the rain, which now you appreciate, because it helps everything to grow. The list is endless. The ability to appreciate your life, even the difficult and painful bits, is a sure signpost that your mindful practice is bearing fruit.

7. Kindness *(moving away from judging)* **and generosity**
All our lives we can feel as though we are being judged. At school we are judged by how well we do in exams. At work we are judged by how much we earn. As parents, we are sometimes judged by the behaviour of our children. We constantly judge ourselves: whether we are succeeding or failing. For many, our parents were the harshest judge of all: and while that judging may have had a good intention, the result is that we feel like we are never good enough.

Judging follows on from complaining: we are looking at what is wrong. When it comes to ourselves, we are experts in all that is lacking: how we don't look attractive enough, how we are not young enough, how we don't work hard enough, and so on. If we look deeply, we realise that our judgments towards ourselves and others are rooted in unkindness: and the result is suffering.

Our habit energy of judging is so ingrained that to try to offer kindness, particularly to ourselves, can feel strange, or even unacceptable. When we practise the kindness meditation in class, students often report that they cannot really offer wishes for well-being to themselves. Isn't it self-indulgent to be nice to ourselves? The truth is this: we don't like ourselves. We believe the judgments that we are not good enough, and therefore it follows that we are not worthy of kindness.

The problem here comes back to the 'self'. Who is this self that I am offering kindness to? If you ask this question for long enough, you will realise that, actually, there is no answer. We don't know who we are. We might have a notion of our personality or our fears or our appearance, but on a deeper level, this 'self' that is me is a total mystery.

Appreciating that mystery is the key to being able to offer kindness and compassion, both to ourselves and to others. As long as we stay on the superficial level of judging (*I don't like the way I look*) then kindness will not be possible. We need to dig deeper, to appreciate the extraordinary fact of our humanity – the fact that evolution has created us, that we are here alive in a remarkable world. Our beings, and indeed all beings, are fragile, temporary and miraculous. Realising this allows our hearts to open, as the following piece explains:

A teacher instructed his students:

When I was conceived, there were many eggs in my mother and thousands of sperm from my father. From all of those possible combinations, only one egg and one sperm survived and came together and grew. What of all the others, that were never born, that never had a chance to live and grow? What becomes of them?

Look outside at the cherry tree. There are hundreds of blossoms, and dozens of fruits will grow and fall, and perhaps only one seed will fall in a place where it can grow. What of all the others, that do not survive, that do not have a chance to live and grow? What becomes of them?

When I see this, I realise that all of these unborn beings did not live, in order that I might live. They did not grow, so that I could grow. I am alive, and living here right now through their grace.

How am I to live my life, so that I honour them?[2]

How do we live, aware of this rare gift of our existence? Each one of us will have a different answer, but one common response is the wish to be helpful and to benefit others. This impulse towards generosity is part of what makes us human, and its effects are profound. In a study done in the United States, half a group of people were given $20 to go out and give themselves a treat, while the other half was instructed to go and give the money away to help someone else. Afterwards, both groups filled in a questionnaire to gauge their happiness levels. The group who gave the money away were significantly happier.[3] What this means is that although we spend a good deal of time trying to make ourselves feel better through shopping and consuming, in the end these activities may not make us happy. We actually feel better when we are thinking of others. It's important to practise generosity not because of what we might get out of it, but because we genuinely wish to help others – so that generosity is another form of loving-kindness. In fact, the more mindful we are – the more we feel connected to the world and everyone in it – the more generosity becomes a natural response.

8. Patience and dedication *(moving away from the quick fix)*
When we start out on any new venture, we want a result as soon as possible. This is partly because the result will inform us that what we've undertaken is worthwhile, which in turn will mean that we are more likely to continue the new regime. These days, there are many self-help techniques all promising instant results.

Mindfulness can also provide rapid results. People often report that their sleep has improved after only a week of working with the body scan. Paying attention to tooth brushing or taking a shower, as simple as it sounds, can be a revelation in terms of coming into the present moment. But there is another, more subtle side to mindfulness, a side that requires immense patience: this is where we are working with the mind.

What happens first, in training the attention, is noticing just how unruly the mind can be. No matter how genuine and wholehearted our intention to stay focused, the mind wanders off, over and over again. If we imagined that we should be able to get the hang of this after a week or two we would, frankly, give up. It's crucial to realise that mindfulness is a lifetime's work. The mind will always wander, and we need to be incredibly patient, like a grandparent with all the time in the world; lovingly inviting it back, over and over and over again. This is the practice. We will never master it. And that is what makes it fascinating.

9. Being a beginner *(moving away from thinking that we know)*

This continuum encompasses all previous categories. In practising mindfulness, if ever you imagine that you completely understand it, or that you have mastered the practice, then you can be fairly certain that you are misguided.

You can tell a genuine orange by the colour and surface of the peel, by the pulp and juice inside, and by the taste. Similarly, a genuine mindfulness student is identifiable through a simple characteristic: beginner's mind.

Beginner's mind means that *we know that we do not know*. It means that we are open and curious, and willing to learn. It means that we appreciate that we don't know what will happen each time we sit down to meditate. It means that we appreciate how subtle and mysterious the practice is. As Shunryu Suzuki, a Japanese Zen Master who went to teach in California in the 1960s, famously said: 'In the beginner's mind there are many possibilities. In the expert's mind, there are few.'[4] The expert is closed, the beginner is open. To practise mindfulness, we really need to be open: open to experience, open to what is not known, open to our own limitations and vulnerability.

Walking the path

In general, the qualities mentioned in this chapter – wholeness, wholeheartedness, curiosity, allowing, experiencing, resilience, gratitude, kindness, generosity, patience, and beginner's mind – appear naturally as we walk on the path of living more mindfully. We don't need to make a special effort: if we just do our best to be present, and to appreciate our life and the people around us, we will inevitably notice quiet changes in our actions and in how we see the world.

One of the criticisms that is sometimes levelled at modern mindfulness training is that it does not include an ethical dimension. No one tells us not to steal, not to harm others, not to speak unkindly, and so on. And yet here is another secret: through the practice of paying attention, these choices (that we are continually making) arise naturally. Learning how to live well, how to cause less suffering to ourselves and others, is inherent in mindfulness practice. The signposts mentioned in this chapter inform us of this reality. No one tells us to be kinder or more resilient: somehow, it just happens.

The
Seventh
Secret

Entering the
Dragon Gate

20.
The Dragon Gate

The woodland roars with savage winds. Close the eyes and listen – it sounds like the crashing sea. But unlike the sea there are lulls, when the tall trees stop being thrashed about, when there is silence. And then it starts up again, like labour, intense and unstoppable, this wild birth of spring.

One day, Dogen, a thirteenth-century Japanese Zen Master, instructed his students:

In the middle of the sea, there is a place where great waves rise known as the Dragon Gate. If a fish can pass this place, it turns into a dragon.

This is why it is called the Dragon Gate. Yet it seems to me that the waves are no higher than those in other places, and the water must be just as salty as anywhere else. Strangely enough, though, any fish that passes this place becomes a dragon without fail. Its scales do not change, its body remains the same; yet it suddenly becomes a dragon.[1]

So somewhere, and we are given neither map nor directions, there is this dragon gate. It is a magical place. *If a fish can pass this place, it turns into a dragon.* This is complete transformation. Dogen adds that the waves are not higher, nor the water any saltier; in other words, this place is like every other place in the sea. And stranger still the fish, when it passes this place, does not change in appearance, and yet, it becomes a dragon. How can this be?

Dogen is, of course, talking about us. You and me, who are on this path of practising (or not practising) meditation. Each one of us is a fish. We are swimming about, doing our best to stay alive, without even any idea of dragons. And then something happens. We pass through this gateless gate. We look the same, but we are changed. Before, we were fish, barely conscious, just doing our best not to get eaten and to find enough sustenance to make it through each day. Now, suddenly we find that we are dragons. We have strength, power, wisdom. We have consciousness, perspective, compassion. We are no longer confined by the sea: we can breathe air and walk on land. How did this happen?

The answer is two-fold, or rather, it is like a piece of paper folded in two; and when we open it out, we realise it is all one piece. The first part of the answer is a question. The question that keeps bubbling up, in the mind, on these pages:

What is your deepest wish?

The curious thing about this question is that it does not require an immediate or definitive answer. It only requires that we hold the question within us, within our hearts, and allow it to be our guide. This question will steer us away from the trivial and the selfish, and towards ourselves, our deeper selves, where we find our innate wisdom and compassion. In other words, this question steers us straight to the dragon gate.

The second part of the fold is practice. When we hold the question about our deepest wish so that we are always aware of it, something extraordinary is likely to occur. This extraordinary event is that we are drawn naturally, almost effortlessly, to practice. And when we practise, when we form the clear intention to notice the gift that each moment of our lives offers us, suddenly, right here in front of us, is the dragon gate. We do not have to go on some special quest to find it: it is here, in the midst of our ordinary lives. It is here, contained within this breath that we taking in, just now. We don't notice, because we are always looking somewhere else, for something else. *But here is the secret: the dragon gate is only present when we are present.* And when we are present, each time we are present, we have already passed through: and on the other side, although there is no outer change, everything is transformed by our wonder. Now, at last, our eyes open to the world, and we are finally awake.

21.
After-story
(within a story)

*The alders are in bud. The spears of yellow flag grow
visibly taller each day. Today, before anything else, lying
down on the small deck outside the hut, and looking
up into the blue sky. A red kite soars on the thermals
with effortless freedom. This morning, for the first time
in many months, the sun feels warm upon the skin.*

Many years ago, someone told me that there was a retreat
going on in my local yoga centre, with a real live Zen
master. Although I was meditating on my own, I had never met
a proper meditation teacher, so I went along. For some reason,
I was the only one there. There was a schedule, so I turned up
each day, and the Zen master, who was called Hogen, turned
up each day, and we spent hours meditating, interspersed
with walking meditation and yoga. He did not speak a word of
English, so we would just bow.

The next year, there was another meditation retreat, and
this time there were lots of people attending. It was my job
to go to the airport and collect Hogen. While we were driving
home, I tried to tell him a story I had read, to explain how I felt
about meditation practice. This is the story:

One time there was a group of students practising meditation
together, and one day a teacher came to offer guidance.

'Meditation,' he said, 'is like filling a sieve with water.' After the teacher left, the students discussed what he meant. Maybe he was telling them they would never understand, as it was, of course, impossible to fill a sieve with water. Maybe he was making fun of them. They all forgot about the teacher, except for one student, who remained deeply perturbed. She couldn't figure out what he had been trying to tell them. So she went to the town where he lived, and asked him what he meant.

The teacher got a metal sieve and a cup from his kitchen, and took her down to the seaside. 'Okay,' he said, 'show me how you fill the sieve with water.' So she took the cup, and scooped up the water as fast as she could to fill the sieve. It was hopeless.

'Okay,' the teacher said, 'now let me show you how I fill it.' The teacher took the sieve, and threw it out into the sea. Together they watched it sink. 'Now,' the teacher smiled, 'the sieve is full of water, and it will always be full of water. In order to practise, you must throw your whole being into it, not just take a sip here and there.'[1]

This is the story I was trying to explain. Hogen, who had been studying English all year, got most of it, but he didn't know what a sieve was. I took him to my house and got a sieve from the kitchen cupboard, and turned on the tap. 'See,' I said. 'The water just goes straight through. It's never full. That's how my practice feels, and I don't know how to throw it into the sea.'

Hogen nodded to show that he understood what I was trying to say, and then put his hands on my shoulders.

'Only look here now,' he said. 'We are *already* in this sea.'

That is all, really. As you hold this book in your hands, this is it. When you finish these sentences, and look up at the world around you, however it is, *this is it*. This is the moment. This is *your* moment, the one being given to you to appreciate and experience. Your life, your deepest wish, your inner path, are all revealing themselves, here ... now. Breathe into it, touch it with your fingertips. Experience it with the whole of your being. You are already in the sea, and the dragon gate is right here, just for you. This is the moment, the only moment you have, to step through.

The doors of the hut are open, at last. The division between inside and outside is gone. Primroses are in bloom, the earth's way of smiling. Birdsong fills the warm, wavering air. A robin hops across the deck on his impossibly thin legs, looking in, as if to say, When will you feed me? When will you feed me?

There can only be one answer: just now, just now.

ACKNOWLEDGEMENTS

The author offers sincere thanks to Coleman Barks for permission to include his translations of two poems by Rumi: 'Who Makes These Changes?' and 'A Little Time Alone in Your Room'. Thanks to the University of Hawaii Press for permission to use the excerpt from Dogen's *Dragon Gate*. The quotation 'There is one thing in this world' is taken from *Discourses of Rumi*, translated by A J Arberry, © Curzon Press 1993, reproduced by permission of Taylor & Francis Books UK. Deep thanks to Hogen Daido Yamahata for permission to use the story 'When I Was Conceived'; and to Public Service Broadcasting in the USA and their programme *Healing from Within* for permission to use Jon Kabat-Zinn's quotation about weaving the parachute. While every effort has been made to contact all copyright holders, if any have been inadvertently overlooked, the author and publisher will be pleased to make the necessary arrangement at the first opportunity.

NOTES

Opening quotation

1. Neville Dowley, yoga teacher and McTimoney Chiropractor, Oxford.

Introduction

1. Jon Kabat-Zinn, quoted from the video *Healing From Within*, presented by Bill Moyers (Public Broadcasting System, USA, 1993).

2. For more on information on the five hindrances, see *In the Buddha's Words, An Anthology of Discourses from the Pali Canon*, edited by Bhikkhu Bodhi (Wisdom Books, 2005), pp. 270–2. Also see www.accesstoinsight.org and search for 'The Five Mental Hindrances'.

3. From the traditional children's song *We're All Going on a Bear Hunt* from the United States.

4. From *Discourses of Rumi*, translated by A J Aberry (Curzon Press, 1993), p. 19.

Chapter 2. Feeling the heat

1. For more on The Four Noble Truths, see *In the Buddha's Words, An Anthology of Discourses from the Pali Canon*, edited by Bhikkhu Bodhi (Wisdom Books, 2005), pp. 75–8.

Chapter 3. Gathering the fuel

1. For more on the autonomic nervous system, see *Why Zebras Don't Get Ulcers* by Robert M Sapolsky (St Martin's Press, 2004), p. 19ff.

Chapter 4. Breathing life into the fire

1. From *Parami, Ways to Cross Life's Floods* by Ajahn Sucitto (Amaravati Publications, 2012), p. 159.

Chapter 5. Introducing obstacles

1. From a lecture given by Jon Kabat-Zinn in Oxford in 2010, and also described in *Mindfulness for Beginners* by Jon Kabat-Zinn (Sounds True, 2012), pp. 115–16.

Notes

Chapter 6. Physical obstacles

1. The arrow analogy comes from the *Sallatha Sutta: The Arrow*, translated from the Pali by Thanissaro Bhikkhu, 1997. For the full text go to www.accesstoinsight.org and search for 'Sallatha Sutta'.

Chapter 7. Attachments and desires

1. *In the Buddha's Words, An Anthology of Discourses from the Pali Canon*, edited by Bhikkhu Bodhi (Wisdom Books, 2005), pp. 270–2. Also see www.accesstoinsight.org and search for 'The Five Mental Hindrances'.

2. J. Rumi, 'Who Makes These Changes?' in *The Essential Rumi*, translated by Coleman Barks and John Moyne (Castle Books, New Jersey, 1997), p. 110.

3. J. Krishnamurti, *The Only Revolution, Europe*, part 12. See: www.jkrishnamurti.org.

Chapter 8. Aversion

1. For more on the subject of Loving-Kindness, see Sharon Salzberg's book *Loving-Kindness: The Revolutionary Art of Happiness* (Shambala Classics, 2002). See also *The Mindful Path to Self-Compassion* by Christopher Germer (Guilford Press, 2009).

Chapter 9. Depression

1. Taken from DSM-IV criteria for diagnosis of depression, which can be found at www.gpnotebook.co.uk

Chapter 10. Unhelpful views

1. From *Epictetus, Discourses and Selected Writings*, translated and edited by Robert Dobbin, (Penguin Classics, 2008), p. 207.

2. Quotation comes from *Only Don't Know, Selected Teaching Letters of Zen Master Seung Sahn* (Shambala Press, 1999).

Chapter 12. Working with resistance: the second key

1. Einstein quotation: '(A human being) experiences himself, his thoughts and feelings, as something separated from the rest – a kind of optical delusion of his consciousness,' in *The New Quotable Einstein*, edited by Alice Calaprice, (Princeton University Press, 2005), p. 206.

2. From a talk given by Thich Nhat Hanh at Plum Village in the summer of 1995. Now available as an audio book entitled *The Ultimate Dimension: An Advanced Dharma Retreat on the Avamsaka and Lotus Sutra* (Sounds True, 2004).

3. To see more on this, consult *Everyday Zen* by Charlotte Joko Beck (Thorsons, 1989), p. 47.

CHAPTER 13. THREE ESSENTIALS

1. From a talk given by Irmgard Schloegl in the 1980s in London.

CHAPTER 14. EFFORT AND EASE

1. To find out more, see www.aaronsiskind.org

CHAPTER 15. THE TOOLKIT

1. From *Full Catastrophe Living* by Jon Kabat-Zinn (Piatkus Press, 1990), p. 61.

2. From *Mudras*, by Gertrud Hirschi (Weiser Books, 2000).

3. From *Religiousness in Yoga* by D V K Desikachar (University Press of America, 1980).

4. From *Anger* by Thich Nhat Hanh (Rider, 2001), p. 24.

5. 'RAIN' is adapted from *True Refuge: Finding Peace and Freedom in Your Own Awakened Heart* by Tara Brach (Bantam 2013).

CHAPTER 16. ABOUT BREATHING

1. For more on this, see *The Breathing Book* by Donna Farhi (Holt Paperbacks, 1996), pp. 48–60.

2. For more on this, see *Hyperventilation Syndrome: A Handbook for Bad Breathers*, by Dinah Bradley (Berkeley, Ca., Celestial Arts, 1991).

CHAPTER 17. WHAT GOES ON IN THE MIND

1. *Default Network* from research by Gusnard and Raichle in *Nature Reviews/Neuroscience* (2001), 2, pp. 685–94.

CHAPTER 18. FINDING THE SUPPORT WE NEED

1. 'Mindfulness-Based Stress Reduction (MBSR) useful in reducing chronic pain' by Jon Kabat-Zinn in *General Hospital Psychiatry* (1982), April 4 (1), pp. 33–47.

2. 'MBSR reduces Blood Pressure' by Joel W Hughes, et al. in *Journal of Behavioral Medicine* (October 2013), 75 (8), pp. 721–8.

3. 'MBSR improves psoriasis' by Jon Kabat-Zinn, et al. in *Psychosomatic Medicine* (September–October 1998), 60 (5), pp. 625–32.

4. 'Meditation reduces thinning of cortex' by Sara W Lazar, et al., in *Neuroreport,* (28 November 2005), 16 (17), pp. 1893–7.

5. 'Mindfulness-Based Cognitive Therapy (MBCT) reduces relapse of depression' by John D Teasdale, et al. in *Journal of Consulting and Clinical Psychology* (2000), 68 (4), pp. 615–23.

6. 'MBCT helps with Generalised Anxiety Disorder' by Susan Evans, et al. in *Journal of Anxiety Disorders* (May 2008), 22 (4); pp. 716–21.

7. 'Mindfulness reduces aggressive behaviour' by Whitney L Heppner, et al. in *Aggressive Behaviour* (2008), 34 (5), pp. 486–96.

8. 'Mindfulness improves the immune system' by R J Davidson, et al. in *Psychosomatic Medicine* (July–August 2003), 65 (4), pp. 564–70.

9. 'Mindfulness reduces amygdala size' by Adrienne A Taren, et al. in *PLoS One* (22 May 2013), 10.1371/journal.pone.0064574.

10. From *The Essential Rumi*, translated by Coleman Barks (Penguin, 1995), p. 260.

CHAPTER 19. SIGNPOSTS

1. From *Start Where You Are,* by Pema Chodrun (Shambala Publications, 1994), pp. 34–5.

2. From a talk given by Hogen Daido Yamahata, Kuwahara, Japan, January 1989.

3. 'Pro-social Spending and Happiness: Using Money to Benefit Others Pays Off' by Elizabeth W Dunn, et al. in *Current Directions in Psychological Science* (February 2014), 23 (1), pp. 41–7.

4. *Zen Mind, Beginner's Mind* by Shunryu Suzuki (Weatherhill, 1970), p. 21.

CHAPTER 20: THE DRAGON GATE

1. *A Primer of Soto Zen* by Dogen Zenji (University of Hawaii Press, 1971), pp. 105–6.

CHAPTER 21: AFTER-STORY (WITHIN A STORY)

1. *Encounters in Yoga and Zen* by Trevor Leggett (Routledge & Kegan Paul, 1982), pp. 39–40.

FURTHER READING

Books on mindfulness

Vidyamala Burch and Danny Penman, *Mindfulness for Health*, Piatkus Books, 2013.

Rick Hanson and Richard Mendius, *Buddha's Brain*, New Harbinger Publications, 2009 (on neuroscience and mindfulness).

Jon Kabat-Zinn, *Wherever You Go, There You Are*, Piatkus, 2004.

——, *Mindfulness for Beginners,* Piatkus, 2012 (includes CD).

Mark Williams and Danny Penman, *Mindfulness: A Practical Guide to Finding Peace in a Frantic World*, Piatkus, 2011 (includes CD narrated by Mark Williams).

Mark Williams, John Teasdale, Zindel Segal and Jon Kabat-Zinn, *The Mindful Way Through Depression*, Guilford Press, 2007 (includes practice CD narrated by Kabat-Zinn).

Other books on meditation

Thich Nhat Hanh, *Touching Peace*, Parallax Press, 1992.

——, *The Heart of the Buddha's Teaching*, Rider, 1999 (for information on the Four Noble Truths and the Eight-Fold Path).

——, *Anger*, Rider, 2001.

Bhante Henepola, *Mindfulness in Plain English*, Gunaratana, Wisdom Publications, 2002.

Shunryu Suzuki, *Zen Mind, Beginner's Mind*, Weatherhill, 1970.

On kindness

Christopher K Germer, *The Mindful Path to Self-Compassion*, Guilford Press, 2009.

Sharon Salzberg, *The Kindness Handbook: a Practical Companion*, Sounds True, 2008.

On stress management:

Gillian Butler and Tony Hope, *Manage Your Mind*, OUP, 1995 (includes cognitive therapy).

Robert M Sapolsky, *Why Zebras Don't Get Ulcers*, Owl Books, 2004.

On breathing:

Donna Farhi, *The Breathing Book*, Holt Paperbacks, 1996.

Website and App with mindfulness practices:

Headspace.com

ABOUT THE AUTHOR

Kate Carne discovered meditation in 1975. Rather by accident, she found that it lifted her out of depression. She trained for many years with Zen Master Hogen Daido Yamahata, both in the UK and in Japan, and has also studied with Jon Kabat-Zinn and Thich Nhat Hanh. She has an MA in Mindfulness and has been teaching mindfulness classes in Oxford since 2004, during which time she has taught more than 50 courses. She has also worked for The Prison Phoenix Trust, teaching yoga and meditation in prisons all over the UK.

For more information on *Keeping Your Practice Alive* courses, and for free downloads of guided meditations, please visit: www.mindfulnessworks.co.uk.

INDEX

acute illness 25–6
adaptability 146–7
allowing, moving away from
    dissatisfaction 144
ambivalence, moving towards
    wholeheartedness 140–1
anger
    bowing to 74–5
    kindness meditation 100–3
anxiety 27
    Ali's story 45
    kindness meditation 100–3
    moving towards curiosity 141–3
appetites 37
appreciating 56, 57
attachments and desires 34–41
    appetites 37
    being too connected 38
    consumer culture 37
    drive to make things better 36–7
    mindful approach to 38–41
    new relationship with time 40–1
    pressure to achieve goals and
        targets 35–6
    problems with attachments 34
    time pressures 35
    'to do' list 35
attention 139–40
autonomic nervous system 15–16,
    115–16
aversion 42–50
    kindness meditation 100–3
    mindful approach 48–50
avoiding, moving towards meeting
    143–4
awareness 123–5

back pain 26
beginner's mind 151
body scan 15, 87–9
    approach to 81
    purpose 88–9
    sleepiness 26
    when to use 89
boredom 43, 81
bowing to your anger 74–5

breathing 114–20
    Angie's story 115
    chest breathing 116
    connection with being 114–15
    diaphragmatic breathing 116–17,
        118–19
    exploring the breath 117–20
    help with depression 55
    hyperventilation 116–17
    issues around breathing 115–17
    number of breaths per minute
        117
    observing the breath 119
    position of the breath 117–18
    using awareness of the breath
        119–20
Buddha
    the eight-fold path 7–8
    the problem of human suffering
        6–8
Buddhist view of mindfulness 18

caffeine 29
cancer, Lucy's story 8–9
chest breathing 116
chin mudra 95, 96
chronic illness 26
chronic pain 26
cognitive adaptability 146–7
complaining, moving towards
    gratitude 147–8
consumer culture 37
cosmic mudra 95, 96
curiosity, moving away from fear
    141–3

dedication, moving away from the
    quick fix 150–1
deepest wish see What is your
    deepest wish?
depression 51–7
    and life's spiral 52–3
    appreciating 56, 57
    breathing practice 55
    dealing with high expectations 55
    definition 52

effects of mindfulness practice
52–3
features of 51–2
how to practise mindfulness 54–7
labelling your thoughts 56–7
mindful walking 56
recognising symptoms 54
Sally's story 57
smiling 56
three breaths practice 55
when to do a mindfulness course 54
Desikachar, D V K 97
desires *see* attachments and desires
diaphragmatic breathing 116–17,
118–19
difficult times, practices for 111–13
discomfort, as source of intention 4
dispersion, moving towards
wholeness 139–40
dissatisfaction, moving towards
allowing 144
Dogen Zenji, Zen Master 155–6
doubts, renewing energy 83–4
Dowley, Neville ix
Dragon Gate 155–7, 160

eating meditation 103–4
Bella's story 103–4
effort
finding balance in meditation
effort 85–6
guitar strings analogy 85
muddy pond analogy 86
ego 69
Einstein, Albert 67
emotions, bowing to 74–5
Epictetus 60
ethical behaviour 152
exhaustion 27, 28–9
experiencing
coping with uncertainty 146–7
moving away from our personal
'story' 144–6

failure, non-judgmental approach to
practice 19
fear
kindness meditation 100–3
moving towards curiosity 141–3
obstacle to practice 43–5
that things will fall apart 46–7

feeling overwhelmed, moving
towards resilience 146–7
'fight or flight' response 15–16, 27,
115–16
Maria's story 142
quietening 142–3
full-length practices 87–103

generosity and happiness 149–50
goals
approaching mindfulness practice 19
pressure to achieve 35–6
gratitude, moving away from
complaining 147–8
groups, supportive energy 131–3

habit energy
and choice of mindful practice 11
awareness of (Adam's story)
13–14
of fixing 36–7
observing 11–12
happiness
and generosity 149–50
understanding what makes us
happy 39–40
hindrances to practice, five
hindrances xv–xvi *see also*
obstacles to practice; resistance
Hogen Daido Yamahata, Zen Master
158–9
hyperventilation 116–17

illness 25–6
mindful approach to 30–3
impatience 47
improvement, drive for 36–7
initialising energy 79–80
inner path 63–5
insomnia 27
bedtime routine 29–30
mindful approach to 29–30
inspiration 129–31
intention
and beginning to practise 17–19
and your deepest wish 19–20
clarity of 19–20, 189
developing and maintaining 5
discomfort as source of 4
non-judgmental approach 19
wholeheartedness 140–1

jnana mudra 95, 96
judging
  feeling we are never good enough
    148–9
  moving towards kindness 148–9
  unhelpful views 58–60

Kabat-Zinn, Jon xiii–xiv, 23–4, 32, 60,
    90, 105
ki gung 97
kindness
  and generosity 149–50
  moving away from judging 148–9
kindness meditation 49–50, 100–3
  Jane's story 101–2
  Saleem's story 102–3
  when to practise 102–3
knowing that we do not know 151
Krishnamurti, J. 41

labelling your thoughts 56–7,
    109–11
letting go 8–9
  limiting the sphere of your activity
    75–6
life's spiral, and depression 52–3
longer practices
  challenges of 14–16
  from doing to being 15–16
  time for stress levels to diminish
    15–16

meditation
  awareness 123–5
  creating a place to meditate 134
  meta-thinking 123, 124
  phases of 121–5
meeting, moving away from
    avoiding 143–4
meta-thinking 123, 124
mindfulness
  Buddhist view 18
  courses 10–11
  of daily activities 105
  secular view 18
  signposts on the path 139–52
  walking the path 152
Mindfulness Based Cognitive
    Therapy (MBCT) 105
mindfulness practice xiii–xiv
  areas of effort 77–8

being mindful in the midst of
    turmoil 82–3
  bowing to your anger 74–5
  breathing 114–20
  choice of mindful practice 4–5, 11
  developing and maintaining
    intention 5
  discomfort as source of intention 4
  getting down to practice 77–84
  getting knocked off course 82–3
  how to start again 83–4
  initialising energy 79–80
  John's story 80–1
  keeping a schedule 73–4
  limit the sphere of your activity
    75–6
  obstacles to overcome xiii–xvii
  practising at home 78–9
  practising with others 131–3
  process of meditation 121–5
  putting the right elements
    together 3–5
  reasons for doing 18
  renewing energy 83–4
  skilful effort during practice 85–6
  sustaining energy 80–1
  three essentials 73–6
  what goes on in the mind 121–5
mindfulness practices toolkit
    87–113
  being with difficulty 112–13
  body scan 87–9
  discovering what works for you 113
  eating meditation 103–4
  full-length practices 87–103
  kindness meditation 100–3
  labelling thoughts 109–11
  mindfulness of daily activities 105
  practices for difficult times 111–13
  RAIN tool 111–12
  seated meditation 89–97
  shorter practices 103–11
  three breaths 104–5
  walking meditation 106–9
  yoga 97–9
multi-tasking, giving up 75–6

negative emotions, kindness
    meditation 100–3
non-judgmental approach to
    practice 19

Index

non-judgmental thinking 59, 60
non-selfing 112

observing 11–12
obstacles to practice xiii–xvii
  as part of practice 23–4
  attachments and desires 34–41
  aversion 42–50
  boredom 43, 81
  depression 51–7
  fear 43–5
  fear that things will fall apart 46–7
  impatience 47
  judgmental thinking 58–60
  physical obstacles 25–33
  rebelliousness 47–8
  restlessness 42–3
  unhelpful views 58–60
outer path 64

pain 26
  mindful approach to 30–3
  Toni's story 32–3
  turning towards 143–4
panic attacks 142
para-sympathetic nervous system
  15, 16, 116
patience, moving away from the
  quick fix 150–1
pausing and observing 11–12
  Clara's story 12
paying attention 139–40
phones, switching off 38
physical obstacles 25–33
  exhaustion 27, 28–9
  illness 25–6, 30–3
  insomnia 27, 29–30
  pain 26, 30–3
  sleepiness 26, 28–9 see also
    insomnia
  tiredness 26–7, 28–9
  working with 28–33
practising with others 131–3
  Dan's story 131–2

quick fix attitude, moving towards
  patience 150–1

RAIN tool 111–12
rebelliousness 47–8
renewing energy 83–4
research into mindfulness 133–4

resilience, moving away from feeling
  overwhelmed 146–7
resistance xiii–xvii
  and the 'to do' list 63–4
  demands of the outer path 64
  importance of the inner path 63–5
  notion of the self 66–70
  the first key 63–5
  the second key 66–70
  The Story of Me 66–70
  what is your deepest wish? 65
restlessness 42–3
retreat
  author's experience 158–9
  going on 135–6
Rumi xviii, 134
  'Who Makes These Changes?' 40

schedule for mindfulness practice
  73–4
seated meditation 15, 89–97
  position of the hands 94–6
  sitting positions 90–4
  sleepiness 26
  when to practise 97
secular view of mindfulness 18
self
  connection with everything else
    67–70
  ego 69
  false notion of being separate 66–7
  feeling we are never good enough
    148–9
  historical dimension 68–70
  image of 66–70
  offering kindness to 148–9
  The Story of Me 66–70, 145–6
  ultimate dimension 68–70
self-compassion 28, 135
selfishness 37
Seung Sahn, Zen Master 60
short practice, benefits of 13–14
shorter practices 103–11
signposts on the path of
  mindfulness 139–52
  allowing 144
  beginner's mind 151
  curiosity 141–3
  dedication 150–1
  experiencing 144–6
  generosity 149–50

signposts (*continued*)
  gratitude 147–8
  kindness 148–50
  meeting 143–4
  patience 150–1
  resilience 146–7
  turning towards suffering 143–4
  walking the path 152
  wholeheartedness 140–1
  wholeness 139–40
Siskind, Aaron 84
sleepiness 26
  mindful approach to 28–9
  see also insomnia
small changes, Adam's story 13–14
smiling 56
social media 38
social pressures 35–6
specific practices 4–5
  choice of 10–11
stress, time to diminish during
  practice 15–16
stress responses 15–16 *see also* 'fight
  or flight' response
stretching 97
Sucitto, Ajahn 19
suffering
  and willingness to change 8–9
  reasons for practising mindfulness
    18–19
  search for an answer to 6–9
  turning towards 143–4
support
  bite-sized practice 135
  creating a place to meditate 134
  Dan's story 131–2
  finding 129–36
  going on retreat 135–6
  inspiration 129–31
  practising with others 131–3
  research into mindfulness 133–4
  Sam's story 135
  self-compassion 135
  teachers who inspire us 129–31
  tuning in to your deepest wish 136
sustaining energy 80–1
Suzuki, Shunryu, Zen Master 151
sympathetic nervous system 15–16,
  115–16

tai chi 97
teachers who inspire us 129–31
Thich Nhat Hanh, Zen Master 64,
  68, 100
this is the moment 158–60
thought labelling 56–7, 109–11
three breaths 104–5
Three Minute Breathing Space
  105–6, 135
time
  creating a new relationship with
    40–1
  making small changes (Adam's
    story) 13–14
  never enough of 12–14
time line of our life 145
time pressures 35
tiredness 26–7
  mindful approach to 28–9
'to do' list 35, 63–4
toolkit of mindfulness practices
  87–113

uncertainty, coping with 146–7
unhelpful views, judgments
  58–60

walking meditation 106–9
walking mindfully 56
wanting, habit of 34
weekly classes 10
What is your deepest wish?
  clarifying intention 19–20, 189
  contacting your inner path 65
  giving direction to practice 156–7
  guide to the dragon gate 156–7
  reflection on 19–20
  tuning in to 136
wholeheartedness, moving away
  from ambivalence 140–1
wholeness, moving away from
  dispersion 139–40

yoga 28, 29, 97–9
  benefits of mindful yoga 97–9
  Joe's story 98–9
  when to practise 99